LOSING
YOUR POUNDS
OF PAIN

Other Books by Doreen Virtue, Ph.D.

The Yo-Yo Syndrome Diet

My Kids Don't Live with Me Anymore: Coping with the
Custody Crisis

The Chocoholic's Dream Diet

LOSING
YOUR POUNDS
OF PAIN

Breaking the Link Between
Abuse, Stress, and
Overeating

Doreen Virtue, Ph.D.

Hay House, Inc.
Carson, CA

Copyright © 1994 by Doreen Virtue

Published and distributed in the United States by:

Hay House, Inc.
1154 E. Dominguez St.
P.O. Box 6204
Carson, California 90749-6204

Editor: Jill Kramer
Typesetting/internal design: Freedmen's Typesetting Organization,
   Los Angeles, CA 90004

The author of this book does not dispense medical advice nor prescribe the
use of any technique as a form of treatment for physical or medical problems
without the advice of a physician, either directly or indirectly. The intent of
the author is only to offer information of a general nature to help you in your
quest for physical fitness and good health. In the event you use any of the
information in this book for yourself, which is your constitutional right, the
author and the publisher assume no responsibility for your actions.

Library of Congress Cataloging-in-Publication Data

Virtue, Doreen, 1958–
   Losing your pounds of pain : breaking the link between abuse, stress,
and overeating / Doreen Virtue.
      p.   cm.
   Includes bibliographical references and index.
   ISBN 1-56170-095-9 : $12.95
   1. Compulsive eating.   2. Obesity—Psychological aspects.   I. Title.
RC552.C65V56   1994
616.85'26—dc20   94-15864
                                                                      CIP

ISBN 1-56170-095-9

99 98 97 96 95   5 4 3 2
First Printing, August 1994

Printed in the United States of America
on recycled paper

To my parents, Joan and Bill Hannan, with love and appreciation

C O N T E N T S

I first decided to write this book four years ago while serving as Program Director of an all-women psychiatric hospital specializing in sexual abuse survivors. Every client was struggling with deep emotional pain: stress, grief, depression, and rage; and dissatisfaction with work, marriage, and life in general. They expressed, "Is this all my life will ever be?" to me in various ways. All of these women had turned to food for comfort, security, and sometimes self-punishment. Many were convinced that if they could only lose the weight, all their pain would be released. What they came to learn was just the opposite: First they had to lose their pain, and then their weight would leave them.

When I initially became a psychotherapist specializing in eating disorders, I was relatively naive to the brutal nature of abusive households. I was fortunate to grow up in a home surrounded by loving and extremely intelligent, metaphysically minded parents. My father is a writer, and my mother is a former Christian Science practitioner and Weight Watchers counselor. Is it any wonder I grew up to be a blend of both their occupations? As a therapist, I've used many of the skills my parents taught me: visualization, affirmations, imagery, meditation, and healthful eating and exercise habits. I used these tools in my twenties to dramatically transform my life from an unhappy existence to one that is something straight out of my dreams today. (But you'll read more about my story later on in this book.)

Anyway, my point is that I had never experienced childhood abuse firsthand, but my clients sure had! Woman after woman described various degrees of childhood abuse ranging from emotional neglect; to being verbally assaulted; to molestation, incest, and rape; to cult involvement. By the time I'd been a therapist for a year, I'd worked with hundreds of women who cried, screamed, and released pounds and pounds of pain. It seemed that every time I'd work with a woman, she'd lose weight. As a result, my case load swelled to capacity with women wanting to lose excess pounds. Every one of these women had used traditional diets, only to regain the weight time and time again.

As a psychotherapist, I worked with clients to discover *why* they were overeating, instead of focusing on *what* they were eating. That was considered a radical approach at the time, but is readily accepted today. I wrote my second book, *The Yo-Yo Syndrome Diet*, based on my research on the link between emotions and overeating.

When I first began speaking and writing about the link between childhood abuse and compulsive overeating, the idea was met with resistance. Today, the idea doesn't seem so far-fetched. However, some therapists working with eating-disordered clients have gone a bit overboard in their treatment styles. It seems that some therapists believe that every eating-disordered client has been sexually abused, even if they have no recollection of the event.

Well, not all compulsive overeaters have been sexually abused! The pain they are carrying, in the form of extra pounds, can stem from a number of sources. Those different sources are described in this book.

On the other hand, there are many abuse survivors who repress and forget their sexual abuse as a means of coping with the horrible trauma. I am deeply concerned that the current media blitz about "false memories" and overly zealous eating-disorder therapists will negatively impact those people who really need help.

The methods I use with abuse survivors who compulsively overeat are detailed in the pages that follow, and I've geared this book to provide both information *and* practical help. In the instances where someone needs more assistance than a mere book can provide, I've clearly stated so. Also, since most of my work has centered around women's issues, this book reflects that focus. *Losing Your Pounds of Pain* is geared for women struggling with overeating stemming from stress, depression, anxiety, relationship problems, and career troubles. But, this book will certainly help men facing these issues, as well. Pounds of pain, after all, have no gender-based barriers!

(However, since the majority of people seeking my help are women, this book uses female pronouns such as "she" instead of the awkward phrase, "he or she.")

As always, the only approach to healing a problem is an honest examination of its symptoms and its roots. Once the pain is identified, it needs to be released. When the pain is released, the pounds will be released, too. Weight loss will follow.

I strongly believe that our true, natural state is to be light in body and light in spirit. We are meant to enjoy ourselves and be happy, even while undertaking our responsibilities. Pain is not supposed to be blindly accepted; it is, instead, a signal that something is wrong and needs to be changed or healed. We are meant to have healthy, normal-weight bodies. This book reveals how you can uncover your true, natural self by shedding the false skin of unhappiness and overweight.

Doreen Virtue, Ph.D.,
Newport Beach, California

ACKNOWLEDGEMENTS

Many people helped make this book a reality. First, I want to thank all the women and men who, as my clients, struggled through hours of therapy to release the pain that was keeping them prisoners of overeating and overweight. Their stories and courage moved me deeply, and provided the basis for the lessons in this book.

Big "Thank You's" to the following people who gave personal and professional rallying, encouragement, and emotional support: Michael Tienhaara, Ken and Jan Hannan, Lee Reynolds, Melinda White, Silvia Aslan, Linda Izzo, Dr. Dean Edell, Marcia Weist, Josie Tienhaara, Charles Schenk, Grant Schenk, Ada Montgomery, Jerry Monsey, Dr. Barbara Kalb-Monsey, Pearl Reynolds, Bruce Nelson, Frank Lee, Jay Geer, and The Bakken 4.

I am especially grateful to Louise Hay for her incredible vision and inspirational accomplishments. She has managed to achieve huge success while helping millions—all the while never letting go of her true self and beliefs. Bravo!

Thank you, too, Reid Tracy, for your enthusiasm, energy, and help in getting this book published. Thank you to Jill Kramer for your editing and belief in this project. A special thank you to Dan Olmos, who was there in the beginning and who will always be there in our hearts. And my appreciation also goes to Christy Allison, Jeannie Liberati, and everyone else on the Hay House staff.

IDENTIFYING
THE ROOT
OF
THE PAIN

INTRODUCTION:
BEYOND THE YO-YO SYNDROME

"The unexamined life is not worth living."
—Socrates

EVERY EXTRA POUND you carry on your body equals a pound of emotional pain you are carrying in your heart. This is a book to help you shed your excess weight by releasing that pain.

If you have been on numerous diets and have found yourself continually returning to old patterns of unhealthful eating, there may be a psychological cause and cure. During the past ten years, I've treated and talked with thousands of women and men who couldn't stop overeating. In the majority of cases, the overeating was brought on by emotionally painful and traumatic events and situations, including incest, rape, the death of a loved one, job problems, financial worries, and so on.

Some painful event was usually triggering distress similar to that of a sharp thorn in a lion's paw. These people had lived with the "thorn" for so long that it seemed normal to them. They wanted to accept the pain as "the way it was." But pain is neither normal nor acceptable, and the human response to pain is to seek relief. Many people use food as relief from such pain.

In this book, you'll learn the steps my clients used to unblock and release their pain. Once the pain is released, the insatiable appetite for food is no longer present. The appetite then normalizes, and weight is naturally reduced. This statement is not an oversimplification, but is based on my clinical experience, as well as well-documented research conducted at respected universities and laboratories around the world.

You'll read about that research in subsequent chapters. Much of the research is brand new; some of it has been in the field for eight or nine years. The case histories of my clients and workshop attendees illustrate how *you* can benefit from these studies.

In my practice, I've been involved with near-miraculous recoveries from compulsive overeating, and I'm thrilled to be able to share the stories of some remarkable women and men who have showed enormous courage in pulling the thorn out of their paws. That act, of course, hurts tremendously—but just for a short time. After the thorn is removed, the pain lessens. The sore may ache somewhat, but as time goes on, it heals over.

As you read this book, you may remember events in your life that you would prefer to forget or not dwell on. I want to state, right here, that I find no value in carrying around pain from the past, or dwelling on abusive childhoods. Many people, unfortunately, use their history as an abused child as an excuse for unfinished educations and lackluster careers.

There is only one useful purpose in digging up the past: to identify self-blame that is keeping you miserable today. The sad fact is that most children blame themselves when they are abused—"I must be a very bad girl to make Daddy so angry with me." When the abused child grows up, she still carries this self-blame.

The primary purpose of this book, then, is to search and destroy any needless self-blame that is holding you back from realizing a bright, light life.

Your True State Is a Normal Body Weight

A happy, content person eats moderate amounts of food and keeps physically fit. Her body may not be model-thin or athlete-tight, but she doesn't strive to be "perfect." The happy person carries body weight that is in proportion with her height, and food is simply fuel for daily energy. Food, to a happy person, is not used predominantly for entertainment or comfort.

Anyone who has suffered through an abusive relationship, a life trauma, or excessive stress automatically seeks a way to feel better. Food can provide shelter and a way to block out awareness of painful memories and uncomfortable emotions. But food is a tool that revictimizes the victim. Being fat carries social consequences that are painful, in themselves.

There is nothing wrong with wanting to lose weight and having a healthy body. As I wrote in my book, *The Yo-Yo Syndrome Diet*, when your weight goes up and down, you really see how the world reacts to obesity. When you are thin, you are accorded more respect, admiration, and attention. Men open doors for you and compliment you. When you are overweight, you almost disappear into oblivion. You are no longer special; you are "average."

The overemphasis on appearances in our society is troubling, but it is not likely to change anytime soon. Scientific research confirms what we've known all along: Those who are thin are accorded preferential treatment. They are more apt to be hired and to receive a higher starting salary than an overweight person. They are viewed as being smarter and kinder.

Overweight people are overtly and subtly discriminated against, both by children and adults. The overweight person is in a cycle of pain. The original painful event—whether it was sexual abuse, emotional abandonment by one's parents, an empty marriage, or mismatched career path—pushed her toward food's comfort. She gains weight, and society punishes her for being fat.

During the ten years that I've done psychotherapeutic work with compulsive eaters, I've listened to countless stories of pain, which encompassed everything from unhappy marriages to severe child abuse.

These frustrated overeaters don't blame their weight on others—far from it. They are simply struggling to find peace of mind but, instead, find life filled with difficulties and emotional pain. This pain results in a mindset leading to compulsive overeating, and this state of mind—a combination of discomfort with one's self, sadness, tension, fear, and repressed rage—is difficult to live with. Although eating brings temporary relief from the anxiety, after the fact there is additional anxiety and guilt, and the prospect of gaining even more weight.

Here's how Rebecca, one of my clients, described this cycle of pain: "I just want to be happy. I don't know *how* to be happy, though. Happiness is almost an abstract concept, you know, something I see in the movies. I've felt it from time to time, like when I was first dating my husband, or when my son was born. To me, happiness means relief from the emptiness and sadness I feel most of the time."

Rebecca remarked that the closest she came to achieving true peace of mind was while eating. "Even then, when I'm eating, I don't feel one hundred percent happy. A part of me is watching myself pig-out, and I'm just disgusted with myself. I know what overeating does to my weight, but sometimes food is the only thing that makes me feel good."

The good news, though, is that Rebecca and others have replaced overeating with other activities that truly lead to peace of mind and happiness. The process Rebecca went through to lose her pounds of pain is detailed later on in this book.

Dealing with Unresolved Issues

Do you struggle with your weight? Do you sometimes feel hopelessly drawn to eat something, even though your mind is screaming, "Don't eat it!"? Do you find that diets and weight-loss programs don't work for you?

If you answered yes to any of these questions, then I'm willing to bet that there is some part of your life that is unresolved. It could be an issue from childhood, or it could be a current situation involving work, finances, or a relationship. Being aware of the situation is a positive first step, but awareness alone won't free you from compulsive overeating.

4 ॐ

In my book, *The Yo-Yo Syndrome Diet*, I discussed the link between emotions and overeating, explaining how stress, anger, boredom, and jealousy trigger intense feelings quelled only by food's presence. I also talked about low self-esteem leading to compulsive overeating, but I just scratched the surface with that book. In *Losing Your Pounds of Pain*, I delve into the deeper factors leading people to engage in desperate eating episodes. Here, I discuss how alcoholism in your family background increases the odds you'll overeat foods containing sugar or refined flour. I also describe research studies showing how traumatic sexual experiences shatter the self-image. For example, a sexually traumatized girl will hide her healthy natural state of sexuality, either by covering her body with fat, or by starving her sexuality away.

This book will trigger unconscious processes that will help free you from your pounds of pain. By mentally answering the questions in some of the chapters, you'll undergo much of the work done in psychotherapy, as the material included is almost identical to that which is covered in my therapy sessions.

Feelings will surface as you read case studies about women similar to you. You may feel uncomfortable or saddened by some of the stories, but these are very valuable emotions that needn't be avoided. I promise you that—just as if you were in psychotherapy with me—the discomfort will be supplanted by feelings of relief and peace. So, go through some momentary discomfort, keep reading the book, and you'll find a rainbow at the end of the path. You're worth the effort.

Different Paths to the Same Destination

I'm awestruck by the clear pattern of pain in compulsive overeaters. I didn't start my career in counseling with the intention of finding this pain. Rather, it unfolded in front of me and made itself perfectly obvious.

Every overweight or weight-obsessed person I've worked with has had the same "Pounds of Pain" mindset I discussed earlier. These people are searching for a sense of relief, peace of mind, and self-acceptance. But, the *way* that they acquired this mindset differs greatly.

Many had traumatic first sexual experiences involving date rape, incest, molestation, fondling, or psychological sexual abuse. Other clients had seemingly normal, happy childhoods, with no abuse or alcoholism. However, it turns out that they were emotionally neglected by parents busy with careers or other personal matters.

Those who now find comfort in food often received little solace from relationships. Growing up, they didn't learn how to extract pleasure from interactions with people. Instead, food or material possessions were their primary love objects.

Annette, a 43-year-old manager and divorced mother of two, told me that she'd always felt ugly, and she never believed men who said they loved her. Instead, Annette expected the men in her life to leave her for another more attractive woman. After all, how could she be pretty with the extra 30 pounds she carried on her small frame?

However, the excess weight wasn't responsible for Annette's low self-esteem, as she discovered in therapy. Her feelings of ugliness were keeping her fat. Through many weeks of therapy and journal writing, Annette came to understand that her uncle's sexual advances at the age of nine had created a hungry monster inside her.

"He would babysit for my sister and me, and he would do things to me, things he'd call 'our secrets'," Annette recalled. "Initially, his advances were on the borderline of being sexual, like giving me a bath or kissing me on the mouth. Then, Uncle Frank began touching my genitals—first on the outside—then he'd put his fingers inside my vagina.

"I remember I was real scared. I was afraid of him. He told me that my parents would have a bad fight and get divorced if they knew about our special secrets. So I didn't tell anyone.

"Now I understand how much the whole situation disgusted me, and how I turned that feeling into self-disgust. I mean, I blamed myself for the whole thing because I didn't make enough effort to stop Uncle Frank. But what could I have done? I was just a kid, but the incest made me feel like a big, fat nothing!"

Annette's perception of being a "big, fat nothing" influenced every aspect of her life. She didn't expect people to like or respect her, so she had few friends. She felt that her parents and siblings had betrayed her by choosing Uncle Frank as her baby-sitter, a situation that led to strained family relations. And her brief marriage, which yielded two sons, ended after Annette discovered her husband's extramarital affair, although her husband ended up blaming *her*: "You never want sex," he had complained.

Food was a friend that Annette found she could count on during her painful life—a companion when she was lonely, an entertaining diversion when she was bored. Yet, Annette longed to have a satisfying relationship with another person, and she believed that losing weight and being more attractive were the keys to drawing love and friendship into her life. So she'd go on diets once or twice a year. But the moment she'd deprive herself of her best friend—food—Annette's feelings connected to the incest—that is, anger, frustration, and self-hatred—would resurface. The diets just functioned as a bandage (not a cure), masking the real reason Annette was overweight. It wasn't until she'd gone through therapy that Annette was successfully able to lose, and keep off, her extra 30 pounds.

Research from such institutions as the University of Manchester (U.K.), Cornell Medical Center, and the University of Oxford show a clear link between sexual abuse and mood disorders, usually depression. The studies further point to overeating as the chief coping mechanism for depressed sexual abuse survivors. In fact, researchers at Cornell reported that obese persons are five times more likely to have mood disorders than normal-weight persons.

Further research from prestigious national and international universities also details the phenomenon underscoring the pound/pain link:

- Ten times as many women as men are victims of sexual abuse, the same female-dominated ratio reported in eating disorders (Devine, 1980).
- One study of 54 obese people enrolled in a weight-reduction program found that their rates for mood disorders and current or past

psychiatric illnesses—mostly depression and dysthymia (clinical depression)—were at least five times greater than those found in the general population (Goldsmith, S. J. 1992).

- Women who experience early (before age 14) sexual intercourse against their wishes are significantly more likely to have eating disorders than those who engaged in initial sexual experiences later in life, and/or in accordance with their wishes (Calam, 1989).
- A history of sexual abuse has been reported to be associated with eating disorders two to four times more often than one would expect to see in the general population (Tice, et al., 1989).
- About 20 percent of American women have eating disorders. I believe the fact that 20 percent of American women are also sexual abuse survivors (Burgess, 1985) is no coincidence.
- Compulsive overeaters report experiencing significantly more life stress than "normal eaters." One study (Strober, 1984) concluded that adolescent overeaters experience 250 times the amount of life stress experienced by adolescents who don't compulsively overeat.

Once a person becomes trapped in a depression-borne eating cycle, it is difficult to escape without intervention. The research findings are clear: Obese and eating-disordered individuals have unhealthy coping mechanisms. It is in this area that this book will do the most good.

In the chapters that follow, you'll discover step-by-step methods designed to decrease emotional hunger and help eliminate eating binges fueled by depression, grief, guilt, anger, or stress.

The primary purpose of this book, of course, is to lower your emotional hunger, and I firmly believe in this statement: The entire problem of overweight stems from this type of unhealthy appetite. If you weren't emotionally hungry so much of the time, you wouldn't be eating so much. And if you weren't eating so much, your weight would be normal.

I've identified four primary emotions leading to overeating: Fear, Anger, Tension, and Shame (FATS, or fattening feelings). These feelings are often symptoms of unresolved stress and abuse. While reading this book, you'll learn how to take Fear, Anger, Tension, and Shame and transform them into Forgiveness, Acceptance, and Trust of your Self. And even better—after you release the pain and the accompanying pounds, you'll put the past behind you and Forget All That Stuff!

But first, I'm going to ask you to recall and delve into parts of your past that you may not want to remember. After all, it's not pleasant to examine pain. However, there is a definite purpose to my request. If you're not compulsively overeating, or aren't displaying symptoms of unresolved abuse (depression, insomnia, relationship difficulties, etc.), then I say, "Forget the past right now, and put it behind you!"

But, if you *are* compulsively eating, and traditional dieting methods have frustrated and failed you, then you need to learn from the past first. Right now, your buried pain is triggering out-of-control eating. I urge you to uncover the pain from the past that robs you of your happiness today, because there is most certainly unresolved anger and distrust created by events in your history. If you are chronically overeating, it is probably the result of anger that you have turned on yourself, and unresolved feelings can leave you feeling depressed, scared, and insecure.

By returning to the original trauma or traumas—even briefly—we'll pull the plug on that unresolved anger. We're going to redirect the anger, outward. Then we're going to work on increasing your trust levels, both in yourself and in others who deserve your trust.

At that point, we're going to release the past and the pain connected to it. The FATS feelings will then be Forget All That Stuff! And when the pain is released, the fat and excess appetite will no longer be needed. You won't be holding on to anger; you won't be holding on to pain. You won't need to mask these destructive emotions with food and fat and, as a result, your appetite will normalize, and your weight will drop.

Although the principles put forth in *Losing Your Pounds of Pain* can be successfully incorporated into any balanced, low-fat, moderate-calorie diet, the book does offer specific dietary and exercise recommendations. These suggestions are based on research on the stress- and anxiety-reducing properties of an exercise program and a balanced, high-carbohydrate, low-fat, low-stimulant (sugar, caffeine, etc.) eating plan. The book also outlines a sample 7-day, 1,200-calorie menu with accompanying recipes.

Healing the Unhappiness

As I write this book, there is a dualistic movement in societal awareness regarding childhood abuse. On the one hand, there is an incredible openness in acknowledging and publicly discussing the topics of incest and rape. However, there is a growing suspicion that therapists are planting ideas in the minds of clients who—because they are supposedly open to suggestion by the therapist—begin to imagine they were abused as children. In other words, the supposition is that the therapist has falsely created the idea of childhood abuse in the client's mind.

News accounts in 1994 of a man's accusations toward a high-ranking Catholic priest added fuel to this combustible topic. The man remembered, under hypnosis, childhood sexual abuse perpetrated by the priest. He publicly accused the priest of sexual abuse, leading to an uproar in both the media and the Catholic community. A lawsuit was filed by the "sexual abuse survivor," but later, the man changed his mind and said that he couldn't verify his memories of sexual abuse. The "memories" were actually products of the hypnosis, suggestions brought about by his so-called therapist.

The news media and talk shows latched onto this topic like angry animals chomping on their prey. "Therapists plant ideas in their patients' minds!" screamed the headlines. "Repressed memories are a bunch of psychobabble garbage!" was the media's unqualified conclusion.

But here's the most important part of that news story, which was buried underneath the "big" story and not sufficiently publicized: *That man's "hypnotist" was an unlicensed person who had neither formal training nor advanced degrees in psychology, social work, or medicine.* In other words, it wasn't a therapist or even a certified hypnotist planting suggestions in that client's mind. It was a lay person with no qualifications beyond the ability to charm or manipulate another person—the same "skills" possessed by a smooth-talking salesperson. We mustn't let this troubling and "exceptional" incident cloud an area in which so many legitimately abused people need qualified help!

While I have seen damage inflicted by inexperienced and misguided therapists, and I have seen many questionable cases involving child abuse, I don't believe false abuse memories are widespread.

Why would someone conjure up a false memory of childhood abuse? To explain away unhappiness? Someone would have to be extremely distressed in order to create such memories. And if the person *is* that unhappy, chances are there was some type of childhood abuse.

A child raised with love, safety, and security will naturally grow into a happy adult because happiness is the natural state of being. Although this type of person will still occasionally experience mood fluctuations, these are normal and often triggered by outside influences and life stressors. Most of the time, however, a well-adjusted person feels content. If someone feels unhappy much of the time, something is definitely wrong.

However, healing the unhappiness doesn't involve blaming others or blaming the past. It does involve understanding and learning from the past. It has to do with acknowledging and examining the extra pain that led to your extra pounds, and then taking the steps to lose the pounds of pain.

Subsequent chapters describe different hurtful situations most often leading to compulsive overeating, and also suggest ways to break the pain/pound link. These hurtful situations range from the severe to the seemingly ordinary, but the effect in the occurrences is the same: compulsive overeating tendencies. Each chapter then explains how these abusive situations lead to overeating, as well as offering detailed self-therapy plans for breaking the pain/pound links. If you have

experienced more than one type of abuse, you'll benefit from reading about and following the suggestions for each type of abuse
you've endured.

In every instance, I've tried to make these suggestions easy to follow. I know how many times I've read self-help books filled with complicated advice that I never got around to applying in any practical
sense. The suggestions in this book, however, are the same therapeutic
assignments I've given my clients over the years. Other recommendations were developed at the workshops that I present across the
country—recommendations that I know have helped workshop attendees lose their pounds of pain.

PERFECT CHILDHOODS
AND OTHER MYTHS

*"The ultimate lesson all of us have to learn
is unconditional love, which includes not only
others, but ourselves as well."*
—Elisabeth Kübler-Ross

Childhood Emotional and Psychological Abuse

VERY OFTEN, when I'm taking a history of a new client, this person will tell me, "I had the perfect childhood. No one hit me, and my parents didn't drink." Now, I'm not a negative person who goes looking for problems when they don't exist. But, whenever someone *in therapy*—especially for depression—claims that she had a "perfect" childhood, I usually find evidence of childhood emotional abuse. Like other "ghosts" of abuse, emotional abuse is intangible and subtle and is usually only uncovered by tracing adulthood problems back to their original source.

Certainly, all parents make mistakes in raising their children. There is no such thing as "perfect parenting." No parent—in the absence of mental illness or substance abuse—deliberately sets out to harm a child. So, right off the bat I want to distinguish emotional abuse from normal parenting, with its attendant ups and downs. The chief distinction is that emotional abuse results in lasting scars and negative changes in personality.

What follows are some examples of a common form of emotional abuse: neglect. However, when reading about the women who have suffered from this form of abuse, stay focused on your own childhood.

If you are a parent, try not to lapse into guilt about your own relationship with your children. Now is not the time to examine your own parenting skills (they were learned); it is the time to look at your own emotional issues. In the long run, it is this focus that will help you feel better about yourself, thus making you an emotionally healthy parent.

Neglected Love

The women you will read about here all suffered from neglect (the most common form of emotional abuse) while growing up. They are not self-pitying, whining women—they are actually proud, self-reliant types. But they are all dealing with the pain of compulsive overeating and relationship problems as a result of this neglect. First, there's Melanie.

> — When Melanie recalls her childhood, she has an image of her mother vacuuming and cleaning—constantly. "Every minute, she was cleaning the house," remembers Melanie. "She was always in a rush and a bad mood because she was cleaning up after my brothers and me. I remember feeling guilty when she'd wash the dishes right after we ate."

Melanie's mother exhibited perfectionistic and compulsive tendencies toward housework. The woman rationalized that she was being "a good mother and wife" by keeping the house spotless. That was a strong cultural notion then, a notion that lives on today. But there's a difference between maintaining a neat, sanitary home and spending every moment scrubbing and polishing. Compulsive housekeeping, like workaholism and other addictions, is a means of avoiding intimacy.

Now, since children require emotional connectedness with their parents, those who are raised by "super housewives" are often confused. In the eyes of the outside world, it may seem that this type of mother is perfect because she keeps an immaculate home and cooks like a

French chef. Yet, children growing up in these households are left with an emptiness triggered by the lack of *emotional* mothering (as opposed to the *physical* mothering they may receive).

As these children mature, they try to fill this void with tangible things such as food, which temporarily makes them feel full and numb; and material goods, which may often be purchased in a compulsive fashion. Others may even use people to fill this vacuum, as is the case when some women "collect" boyfriends instead of engaging in one monogamous, intimate relationship.

All of these women have characterized their lives as empty, incomplete, or unfulfilled. They had turned to eating compulsively in an attempt to fill the void left by a lack of emotional or psychological nurturing, but the effort was futile because feeling full from food only temporarily numbs the emptiness inside—after the food digests a bit, the emptiness returns. And with it comes a feeling of self-disgust for having gone on yet another eating binge. Read about more women who suffered from neglect.

— Wanda was neglected by a stay-at-home mother who was usually passed out on the couch, dead drunk, when the little girl got home from school. Wanda had to entertain herself, since she was too embarrassed to invite friends to the house. One time, she even had to clean up her mother's vomit from a drinking binge. Wanda's mother was physically there, every day, but her mother was never really there for her emotionally.

— Edwina's mother, like Wanda's, was chemically dependent. But Edwina's mother denied she had any problem because the drugs she used were prescribed by her doctor. Nonetheless, the tranquilizers made her moods unstable, and she'd often scream at Edwina and her sister for inconsequential reasons. Most of the time, though, Edwina's mother stared blankly in front of her in a drug-induced stupor.

Joyce's pain is known far too well by far too many women. Though not technically abuse, I'm putting her case in this section because it is so widespread.

— Joyce never felt she got enough from her father. She now seeks out aloof and unemotional men who remind her of him. Unconsciously, she is seeking her father's love and approval through them. She tries to change these distant men into warm lovers, believing that if she tries hard enough, they will change. Not surprisingly, Joyce ends up leaving these men because her emotional needs are unmet.

Now, I'm not blaming all fathers for this common scenario by saying that they're "bad" or that they perpetrated this type of behavior on purpose. But many women feel empty or wounded because their fathers didn't express enough love, affection, and approval to them.

— In Mary Ann's case, her father suffered from manic depression, a mental illness that can wreak havoc on family members. One minute, her father would be an energetic, charismatic "buddy-type" dad, and the next minute he'd totally isolate himself behind his bedroom door. Mary Ann never knew what to expect from her father's mood swings, so she constantly walked on eggshells just in case Dad was in one of his moods. To this day, she has difficulty relaxing around male authority figures.

— Angela was the oldest of five children. Since her mother was bed-ridden with a debilitating illness, Angela was the family caretaker. She neglected her schoolwork to shop and cook the family's dinners, and she made sure her mother was cared for. Angela also looked after her younger siblings, coaching them to do their homework, while her own remained unfinished.

Angela's adulthood followed the same course: she took

care of everyone but herself. "Taking care of others is the right thing to do," was her deepest belief, along with the fear of "seeming selfish" if she did anything nice for herself. While being kind, thoughtful, and loving are virtues that many of us try to uphold, Angela's situation was quite different.

Deep down, Angela resented others. She resented them for "taking advantage" of her niceness and also because no one took care of *her* needs. She used food as her weapon to fight back, along with the frequent arguments she had with her husband.

When Angela's weight topped 200 pounds, she finally sought help. In therapy, Angela learned how to balance her desire to take care of her family with her desire to get her own needs met. She discovered how to enjoy simple pleasures such as taking the kids to the park or baking bread with her daughter. Instead of resenting her caretaking activities, she began to appreciate them.

Angela redefined the word *selfishness* and began taking time for herself. The result was that both Angela and her family benefited from her new perception of life. She became a happier, more satisfied wife and mother—definitely more easygoing and fun to be around. She lost weight through her exercise program, and as her appetite lessened, her resentment and frustration level diminished.

— Like Angela, Rosie felt she'd missed her childhood. An only child, Rosie was raised by a single mother who decided that her daughter would be her best friend and mentor. Rosie's mother shared intimate details about her relationships with men, and consistently asked Rosie's advice on love matters.

Unfortunately, Rosie was emotionally unprepared to function as her mother's peer. She needed to *be* mothered, not *act* as a mother. What Rosie's mother did is called "parentifying" her child. In other words, she was pressuring her child to take on the role of the parent. Parents who are emotionally immature, chemically dependent, or who have personality disorders such as narcissism commonly parentify their children.

For Rosie, insufficient parenting produced anger and sadness and the feeling that she'd been "ripped off" from having a real childhood. She despaired about her lack of a normal mother-daughter relationship and, as an adult, resented it when her mother asked for small favors such as a ride to the doctor or store. Her sentiment was, "I don't want to take care of her! After all, she didn't take care of me all those years!"

Instead of confronting her mother with her feelings, though, Rosie kept them to herself. She ate to feel better, primarily binging on "comfort foods" such as breads, cookies, mashed potatoes, and cheeses. The textures of these foods, combined with mood-elevating properties in carbohydrates (more about this in later chapters), pacified Rosie temporarily. But in the long run, Rosie's harbored anger and grief resulted in her overeating 45 extra pounds onto her body.

In contrast, Jean's situation doesn't involve abuse or neglect in the strictest sense. But I've included her story in this chapter, as well as the one that follows Jean's, because they both illustrate other ways in which parents inadvertently prompt overeating.

— Jean's mother was the picture of a sweet, loving woman. She doted on her children, spending hours playing and talking with them. Jean learned a lot from her mother, not the least of which was the pleasure and rewards associated with eating. You see, Jean's mother equated food with love—a connection she learned from her own mother, and she then passed this idea on to Jean.

Whenever Jean would do anything well, such as bringing home an *A* on a report card or cleaning up her room, she would be rewarded with food. There were M & M's for completing her homework on time, cupcakes for vacuuming the living room, and potato chips for walking the dog.

As an adult, Jean wasn't able to break the food-as-reward connection until she got into therapy. Prior to therapy, every time she'd try to diet, she'd feel deprived, which made sense to her once she came to understand the significance she'd placed on food: To Jean, since food was a reward, then diets represented a form of punishment.

— Charlene also learned to overeat as a child. The youngest of 11 children, Charlene's family was constantly struggling to make ends meet. At dinnertime, there never seemed to be enough food, and the moment that dinner was served, Charlene's older brothers would fight to see who could eat as much as possible. As a result, Charlene learned to scramble to get her share of the meal.

As an adult, she entered therapy with me in an effort to understand her compulsive overeating habits. Once she acknowledged her deep-seated fear that "there won't be enough food for me to eat," she was able to curtail her eating. After all, as a parent with a small, financially secure family, Charlene was now able to eat as much food as she wanted. (Unfortunately, she had done just that and gained 75 pounds after marriage.) However, as she worked on releasing the fear that she'd go hungry unless she stuffed herself with food, Charlene gradually lost her excess weight.

— Michelle was also taught unhealthy early childhood lessons about food's purpose, but in a different manner than Jean or Charlene.

Both of Michelle's parents were highly ambitious entrepreneurs. Her father was in charge of sales and marketing for an international pharmaceutical manufacturer—a job that required extensive travel—and her mother was a successful real estate broker who worked seven days a week. During her rare moments at home, Michelle's mother was usually on the telephone setting appointments and closing deals.

Michelle was an only child ("I always wondered why my parents bothered to have a child, since they were never around") who was raised by a housekeeper. "My memories of my parents are seeing them between business trips and appointments," Michelle remembers.

Perhaps to assuage their guilt, Michelle's parents showered her with expensive gifts and clothing. Unfortunately, even though all her material needs were met, Michelle was hungry—emotionally hungry. She was unwittingly taught to fulfill her normal human needs for love and affection with material objects. If she was lonely, she'd turn to her dolls, makeup table, or the refrigerator in order to feel better.

As she matured, Michelle found that she had difficulties with men—as soon as a relationship started to get serious, she'd break it off. Her fear of intimacy was intermixed with an intense desire for love and security. But since she'd never learned how to interact with people, Michelle's closest friendship was with the food she binged on.

Her weight fluctuated by 30-pound swings throughout her adult life, until she got into therapy and worked on her fears of intimacy.

— Patty was a remarkable woman who reminded me of the song, "Tears of a Clown." She was one of those bubbly, effervescent people who is constantly smiling and doing things to please others. I believe that Patty genuinely enjoys making others smile and laugh. At work, she's everyone's favorite co-worker—taking time to listen, bringing in homemade cookies, remembering everyone's birthday.

The only problem was that Patty wasn't taking time to make herself happy, and that's why she entered therapy. Her childhood was a remarkable story of survival. As the oldest of two sisters raised by a promiscuous, alcoholic mother who would regularly leave the children alone to fend for themselves, Patty remembered many instances where, as a young child, she'd have to figure out how to feed herself and her sister. If there was no food in the house, the hungry little girl would have to beg neighbors for meals.

Sometimes her mother would pile the little girls in the car and take them to bars. Patty and her sister would wait in their locked car for hours while their mother sat in a bar getting drunk and looking for boyfriends.

They lived in a run-down, unkempt house, and Patty was too embarrassed to invite friends over. She also felt "less than" the other children at school. Her whole childhood was marked by neglect and abandonment. Even more disheartening was how Patty dealt with her trauma: she blamed herself. Instead of being angered by her mother's alcoholic behavior, Patty felt that her mother was justified in mistreating her. "If I had been a better girl, my mom would have been home more," was the way Patty recalled her childhood. Sadly, children often take responsibility in this way for their parents' behavior.

Unfortunately, Patty grew up feeling responsible for everyone else's welfare and happiness. She reluctantly complained to me that she felt overworked at her job, and that she was working more overtime than she cared to. When we examined the root cause of her overburdened feelings, I wasn't too surprised to discover that Patty had volunteered to complete a female co-worker's paperwork each afternoon. This selfless act allowed the co-worker to leave the office early to meet her boyfriend for dates, but since Patty wanted this woman to like her, she took on more work than she was capable of handling.

Patty's martyrdom led to time inequities for herself and her family. She'd get off work at 6:00 or 6:30, rush to the grocery store, and try to have dinner ready by 7:30. With no free time, Patty never exercised, and she overate to unwind from the day's stress. No wonder Patty was unhappy with the 75 extra pounds she carried on her 5'2" frame.

Reframing Neglect and Abuse

Therapy for Patty consisted of "unlearning" the lessons she had learned in childhood. As an adult, she had to objectively step back and view her mother's behavior as stemming from the disease of alcoholism. Once Patty *understood*—not just intellectually, but emotionally—that even if she had been a perfect child, her mother still would have behaved in the same fashion, Patty quit blaming herself.

What follows is a therapy session that I had with Patty, in which we started to work through her buried feelings connected to her mother's abandonment:

Therapist (me): Patty, I'd like to ask you to think about your own daughter, April, for a minute. She's ten years old, which is about the age you were when your mother began leaving you alone, right?

Patty: Yes, that's right.

Therapist: Can you describe what it would be like if you left April alone and went off on a two-week vacation with your husband?

Patty: You mean without a babysitter?

Therapist: That's right, April would be completely alone in the house for two weeks.

Patty: But—I mean—I would never . . .

Therapist: And, what's more, during that two weeks, you wouldn't leave much food in the house, and you wouldn't leave any money for her.

Patty: But—

Therapist: You also wouldn't tell any of the neighbors to look after her, and you wouldn't call to check on her.

Patty: Why would I do something like that?!

Therapist: In addition, you wouldn't tell April where you were going or how she could get a hold of you during an emergency.

Patty: That's absolutely crazy! Nuts! I can't understand why you would even ask me to think about something like this!

Therapist: Please tell me how that imaginary scenario is any different than what you went through when you were April's age.

Patty: Well, it is different. That was very different.

Therapist: How was it different?

Patty: Well, I was a lot stronger than April is.

Therapist: Really?

It took quite a bit of discussion before Patty's years of denial and defense of her mother's behavior caught up with her. And when it did hit, it hit her hard. Patty tearfully acknowledged, "I can't believe my mother would actually do something like that to us!"

In the process of working with clients who have endured childhood abuse and abandonment, I've witnessed this sequence of events countless times. There is real griefwork involved in mourning the loss of a happy, safe childhood. Here are the steps involved with that griefwork:

1. Remember the events. It's helpful to write them down in narrative form (as if you're telling someone a story).

2. Step back from the situation and view it objectively. The easiest way to do this is to put another child—your own child, for example—in your place. Imagine that child enduring the things that you went through.

3. Ask yourself: how much is this child responsible for the abuse or abandonment? How much is the adult responsible for the abuse or abandonment?

4. Once the answer comes to you, pay attention to your feelings. You may experience feelings of intense anger toward the adult. Don't shut the anger down, no matter how scary it feels to you. This anger, held inside of you all these years, is the primary source of your overeating and any depression that is nagging at you.

5. Let the anger out. Talk about it with a trained professional— someone who will just listen and not offer any advice or try to "console you." Put your thoughts about your anger on paper. But stay focused on the source of your anger—don't allow yourself to turn the anger back on yourself. Many clients I've worked with "shut down" their anger by focusing on their own children and wondering, "Gee, have I been a bad parent myself?" Right now, focus on your own childhood. In the long run, releasing this anger will make you a more effective, happier parent.

The main fear with respect to anger is that you will "lose control" and act out of rage. Many clients have expressed a fear that their anger will make them tear down a building or beat someone up. Don't worry—pent-up anger is much more dangerous than released anger. You won't lose control.

6. As I've stated before, blaming your parent won't solve anything, and it may make matters worse. Even though your parent or other adult perpetrator acted irresponsibly toward you, it's preferable to view this person as "sick," rather than "bad." You'll feel more settled if you reframe your childhood in these terms. Otherwise, you'll resent your parent for the rest of your life, and the resentment will eat you alive. It's better to feel pity than hate.

The bottom line is this: Unleash yourself from feeling responsible for your childhood pain. You were a child, innocent and naive. The pain was inflicted on you by a sick—mentally ill, depressed, or chemically dependent—adult. You did not cause the abuse or neglect. You certainly did not deserve it. And, now that you are an adult, you don't need to carry the burden of childhood pain any longer.

You can release the pain. It's okay to feel good about yourself!

Healing the "Raggedy Ann Syndrome"

Many people who were abused during their childhood feel that they carry the equivalent of a "scarlet letter" around their necks.

Patty remembered being called "white trash" by the mother of a childhood friend, and she mentally shouldered the burden of that label well into adulthood. Even though she and her husband lived in a respectable neighborhood with a very comfortable income, Patty couldn't shake her feeling of being "less than."

"It's like others can see right through me," Patty told me. "Even though I drive a nice car and wear nice clothes, I still feel like that raggedy little girl wearing outfits bought at the Salvation Army."

Do *you* ever feel that way? As if you're somehow "damaged" or "not as good" as others? This phenomenon is what I call the "Raggedy Ann Syndrome." It means that you are hanging on to an outdated image of yourself. You are owning, and taking responsibility for, a false picture of who you are as a person.

You are not damaged. You are a complete and perfect person. You are lovable, and deserving of the respect of others. It's so important not to waste the precious time remaining in your life by hanging on to pain that happened in the past. I'm not asking you to forget the past or pretend it didn't happen. (Unfortunately, repressing a memory only adds to the pain; it doesn't lessen it.)

Instead, I'm asking you to understand your past. First, understand it intellectually by allowing the memories to surface. Next, understand it emotionally by seeing that you—as a little girl—were not responsible for the actions of those adults or older children who hurt you. See the situation in the bright, clear light of reality.

Then, wipe your slate clean and start over. Know that there is nothing wrong with you. Go even further, and see how the pain you endured has actually made you an empathetic, caring, and understanding individual.

Perhaps, like many abuse survivors, you've turned your painful lessons into a benefit for society. The majority of the abuse survivors I've worked with have become helping professionals: nurses, therapists, teachers, and social workers. However, part of the reasoning behind this career choice is based on unhealthy needs, and part on healthy needs.

If you want to help others as a way of avoiding your own pain, that is unhealthy. If you want to help others because you feel you are responsible for making others happy or whole, that is not healthy either.

But if you want to help others as a way of making sense out of your own pain—wonderful! This is a root principle in the philosophy called "Existentialism." Existentialists believe that pain is an inevitable part of being human. A lot of the pain, these philosophers say, has to do with the knowledge that we will inevitably die and then be "nothing."

They say that the best way to deal with this pain is to, first, acknowledge its existence. In other words, admit to yourself that you fear your life will be meaningless. Then, say the Existentialists, you must do something about it. You must *create* meaning in your life.

For myself, my clients, and many of my friends, the way that we've created meaning in our lives is through practical application of the lessons that pain has taught us. For example, I suffered through two devastating child custody battles many years ago. The pain was tremendous, especially when at one point my ex-husband took our two sons and left the state with no forwarding address. For a time, I had no idea where my children were. I also suffered when others blamed me for the divorce and resultant custody battle.

I could have dealt with my emotional pain by turning it on myself and becoming depressed. Actually, for a short time, I *did* start to compulsively overeat and gained 30 pounds during the custody battle. Fortunately, I recognized what I was doing and turned the situation around.

I went to the bookstore and looked for a self-help manual that would ease my pain while I fought to be reunited with my children, but there were no books on the topic. I was unpublished at the time, and only held a two-year associate's degree in psychology. But I promised myself, "If I get through this custody situation, I'm going to write a book. I'm going to use the lessons I'm learning to help others survive the pain."

The pain was, indeed, intense, but eventually my ex-husband and I settled our differences, and today, many years later, we have an amicable joint custody arrangement. I went on to interview hundreds of other mothers and fathers in various stages of custody battles, and compiled the stories of emotional pain that they shared with me (along with my own story) into a book called *My Kids Don't Live with Me Anymore: Coping with the Custody Crisis.*

I think you get my point: You can choose to see your pain as an enemy or a teacher. I was involuntarily schooled in "what it's like to go through a child custody battle" because I went through it myself. Now, I could have hidden this painful lesson from others—believe me, the societal scorn I felt during this period made me feel embarrassed to even admit that I was engaged in a custody battle. Instead, I decided that my circumstances had made me uniquely qualified to write a book to help others.

The paradox of this whole situation is that the child custody battle was the most painful thing I've ever endured in my life. I felt excruciating sadness, fear, guilt, embarrassment, and anger—more than I'd ever weathered before or after.

Yet, writing that book also provided me with one of the greatest highs of my life. The writing process—both for my kids, who helped me with one of the chapters—and myself, was extremely cathartic and healing. The publicity tour afforded me the opportunity to meet other parents across the country. And the letters I've received from mothers and fathers who have been helped by the information in that book have touched me in innumerable ways.

Pulling Yourself Up

When I first decided to write about my child custody experiences, I wasn't sure I could do it. I didn't really believe in myself that much, but I forced myself to try. The first four publishers I submitted the book to rejected it right away. I then told myself, "Oh, well, you weren't meant to be a writer," and I put away the manuscript in a drawer.

It was only months later, when Pepperdine University invited me to speak on grieving and custody loss at an international conference of therapists, that I thought, "I guess there is some interest in this topic." I pulled out the manuscript again, and this time, sent off 30 copies to 30 publishers.

I got 25 rejections, BUT I also received 5 acceptances! I made myself move forward even when I didn't really believe in myself 100 percent. And it worked!

You can achieve *your* goal of ridding yourself of your pounds of pain in a similar fashion!

As you know, pulling yourself up and making yourself "go for it" is like swimming against the tide. Not only do you have your own Raggedy Ann Syndrome to contend with, but, as an overweight person, you must also buck societal intolerance. (We'll discuss fat prejudice in more detail later on.) For now, I just want to assure you that I realize how difficult it is to feel good about yourself when you've got negative forces penetrating your self-esteem.

You've got to start somewhere, though. Giving up and saying, "What's the use? I'll always be fat and miserable," only guarantees one thing: You'll always be fat and miserable. Of course, it is possible to be overweight *and* happy. But, in most cases, if you are truly happy, you will naturally lose excess weight because you won't be emotionally hungry so much of the time!

So, let's slowly begin to turn the tide in favor of YOU. You're working through your pounds of pain by recognizing the childhood trauma you suffered, then releasing feelings of guilt and self-blame. Then, you're letting out pent-up anger, and projecting that anger away from yourself toward the appropriate source. You are acknowledging the adults who were responsible for mistreating you, but instead of blaming them, you are seeing them as sick individuals in need of help. The important thing to remember is: Don't be angry at yourself, and don't sustain resentment against your abuser.

Release the negative feelings. Now. There's never going to be a perfect time to get on with your life and feel better about yourself. Although this process is a struggle and not particularly fun to deal with or think about, you are actually investing in your future by working on these issues right now.

Keep going.

BREAKING OUT OF
SELF-MADE PRISONS

"To thine own self be true."
—William Shakespeare

Married to Pain

I'LL OFTEN work with a client looking for the source of her pain, and witness a near-miraculous occurrence. When the emotions connected to the pain are reframed, and the victim turns the anger outward toward the perpetrator or the situation—and then releases that anger—it's like removing a nail from a tire. The excess weight deflates right before your eyes.

Let me tell you about Cindy as an example.

The 43-year-old brunette schoolteacher came to me to lose the 100 extra pounds she carried on her 5'4" frame. Cindy was a sweet-voiced woman, intelligent and poised. As she spoke with tight lips and a clenched jaw, I sensed tremendous anger in her voice, mannerisms, and vocabulary. There was a sarcastic edge to her stories, which contrasted oddly with the schoolmarm sweetness she'd carefully cultivated. This was clearly a very tense woman who overate in order to stay calm.

Cindy's husband of 18 years, Ralph, was a traveling salesman who would come home only on weekends. Cindy and Ralph slept in separate beds and had stopped having sex ten years before when Ralph admitted to a one-night stand while on a sales call. Not surprisingly, both Cindy and Ralph began putting on weight soon after the admission of infidelity. They were sublimating anger, resentment, bitterness, and unmet sexual needs through overeating. Both were avoiding dealing with the issues central to their marriage.

Cindy had been contemplating divorce since Ralph confessed to his adultery, but she kept postponing making a final decision. For ten years, Cindy had been seesawing over the "should I or shouldn't I?" question concerning divorce. On the one hand, Ralph brought in a healthy income, and his absence during the week allowed her plenty of time for leisure activities and relaxation. And, she rationalized, with all this extra weight on her body, she probably couldn't find a replacement husband very easily. But on the other hand, her marriage was now an empty sham, a marriage of convenience—without even the joy of sex. She and Ralph were more like roommates than marriage partners.

As I've said before, I see divorce as a last-ditch solution to marital problems. It is wise for a couple to try counseling before deciding to separate, especially if children are involved. Fortunately, in Cindy and Ralph's case, that was not an issue. I urged Cindy to bring Ralph in for marital counseling sessions, and I even agreed to arrange for a second therapist to provide counseling in case Cindy wanted to keep me as her own separate therapist. But Ralph refused to come in, even for a weekend session.

Gradually, I watched the inevitable happen: Cindy decided to ask Ralph to leave home for good. I supported Cindy through her difficult decision and helped her go through the painful grieving process. What was remarkable was that as soon as she decided unequivocally that she was "absolutely, positively divorcing Ralph," Cindy's weight started dropping off like a swiftly deflating beach ball.

Her figure changed from unshapely and round to svelte and attractive because she had taken the nail out of her tire, removed the thorn from her paw.

It's important to note, though, that this wasn't a simple cause-and-effect situation like, "Get a divorce, lose 100 pounds." Cindy experienced the typical grieving process associated with this massive life change and the loss of her "roommate," and she worked hard in therapy to honestly confront her wide range of feelings. What made the situation a little more palatable was that Cindy had been emotionally prepared for the divorce, which helped to alleviate her grief considerably. Also, the fact that Ralph was agreeable to the divorce (he was also ready) made the transition easier to endure.

Basically, Cindy lost weight by becoming honest with herself. She overcame her fears of losing Ralph and admitted that they both had to shed their deadened sham of a marriage.

We all have, deep inside of us, a picture of what our life is supposed to be. If our actual existence sharply differs from that dream life, we experience internal conflict—that is, we make ourselves sick or eat or drink too much when we avoid *admitting to ourselves that our life is very different from our fantasies.*

For Better or Worse?

I remember when my own life was a nightmare, far removed from what I had envisioned it to be. You may remember me telling you earlier that I grew up in a warm, loving household and that my first experience with abuse—of the emotional, verbal, and psychological variety—was when I was in my early twenties. I was a relatively uneducated housewife, married to a man who screamed at me. He berated me for everything from my not having the coffee ready on time to my taking too long to go grocery shopping. Nothing I did was right, and my self-esteem hit rock-bottom.

No wonder I was fat! I overate in order to quell the voices deep inside of me, the ones screaming, "This isn't what your life is supposed to be! Get out now!" I found that if didn't eat to excess, I would become all too conscious of the deep emptiness, the incredible sadness, that surrounded my life and marriage.

Now, there's nothing shameful about being a housewife, and nothing wrong with not having a college degree. It's just that *I* wasn't happy in this circumstance. Deep inside, I could envision the life that would make me happy as if I were watching it on television: I was supposed to have a peaceful, calm marriage like my parents, and as far as a career was concerned, I felt that I was supposed to write self-help books that combined my metaphysical upbringing in Christian Science and Religious Science with a new understanding of medicine and psychology. I also "knew" that I was to write while living near the water, and that my body was supposed to reflect happiness and health at a normal weight.

I had a lot to change!

At that time, I had very little belief in myself. My husband's incessant put-downs and the added burden of never having enough money had eaten away at my self-esteem. Even though I had achieved top grades in school and had even skipped the fifth grade, I felt very stupid. I kept thinking, "If I were really smart, I wouldn't be so broke and unhappy!" And we were very, very impoverished—barely able to make the rent, and paying the utility bills every month just in the nick of time before the electricity and phones were due to be shut off. At times, we lived on potatoes and macaroni because we couldn't afford anything else.

I felt ugly, stupid, and incompetent. My husband had done a great job of convincing me that no other man would want me, so I might as well stick with him. He was slowly poisoning my whole life, and I had to escape somehow!

Life Is But a Dream

I had dreamed of being a psychologist and writer, but how could I dare to believe that I could achieve such lofty goals? It almost seemed as if authors were genetically different from people like me, as if they'd been born with some chromosome enabling them to get published. Yet, that fire inside me wouldn't stop burning, pushing me, urging me, to change my life to coincide with my dreams. In essence, I realized that I had two choices: stay in my current situation and get fatter and more miserable, or start working toward that vision of authoring books by the water.

Maintaining the mental picture of where I was going was an important first step for me. Each of us has a mission or purpose, and deep inside, we know what that purpose is. I believe that God has plans for us before we're born, and He makes sure we're equipped with the tools to fulfill His mission. We can "perceive" this mission if we listen very closely.

Of course, everyone's life purpose doesn't involve fame or fortune. I had one client who said his goal in life was to be the world's best tire changer. He meant it!

If you even have a glimpse of what your purpose is supposed to be, it's like a thread you can yank on that will lead you closer to your "big picture." Pull on this thread through solitary meditation, perhaps while walking, exercising, or showering. Concentrate on the mental picture of your dream life until you can see all the details. Don't force the picture to come into focus. Allow it to rise to the surface until it "clicks," and you know this is truly something coming from deep inside of you.

The next thing that commonly occurs after a vision of a dream life appears is that negative thinking rears its ugly head. In my case, I kept thinking, "I'm not special enough to ever get published," and "College will take too long," and "How will I ever be able to afford to live near the water?"

All these negative thoughts were lies that I had accepted as truth. I had to remind myself that God wouldn't have given me my dream if He hadn't also given me the tools to fulfill it. I had to believe in His strength, because I didn't seem to have much of my own at that time.

So, I used affirmations to boost my self-esteem. I couldn't afford to buy an affirmation tape at the store, so I created my own. Now I know that that was the best thing I could have done: Research attests to the power that our own voice has on our unconscious. I was also able to personally tailor the affirmations to fit my personal dreams and goals.

I improvised affirming thoughts on that cassette tape, and put down every dream I could think of, from my desire to have a great figure, to my intention of living near the water. The most effective way of affirming something, of course, is to declare your intention as if it is already a reality. It's the "act as if" principle. So, instead of saying, "I would like to have a great figure," you say, "I *have* a great figure."

Affirmations are also always stated in the most positive terms possible. For example, one would say, "I enjoy eating healthful foods," as opposed to the negatively worded phrase, "I don't like junk food." They both make a similar point, but the former affirmation programs your unconscious much more powerfully than the latter. (In chapter 11, you'll find affirmations that you can incorporate into your own tape.)

Anyway, I listened to the tape I had made two or three times a day. At first, all my negative thoughts came rushing forward. I'd listen to an affirmation such as "I am a bestselling author," and my unconscious would say, "Oh, this is so stupid; it will never work." My negative thinking was like an out-of-shape muscle groaning in response to a strenuous exercise program. But I kept going.

Gradually, I found myself spontaneously "hearing" my affirmations during the day. I'd be doing housework, and I'd think, "I deserve good"—a thought that came straight from my tape! By the fourth week of listening to my affirmations, I was clearly seeing that it was possible to transform my life. Yes, I was still a little scared, intimidated, and unsure—a product of the emotional abuse my husband had inflicted upon me—but I forced myself to persevere, believing that I really had no other choice. At times, I almost felt that I was being led down a dark hallway and simply had to trust that I would be safe when I reached my destination.

The result of my efforts was that my weight began to drop dramatically as I let go of nervous nibbling and stress snacking. However, as my figure improved, my husband became jealous and suspicious. He was certain that I was losing weight to attract another man, but I didn't allow his insecurities to cloud my own vision.

I enrolled in college and soon received my first *A*. I was shocked because I had forgotten I was smart! I had replaced the true picture of myself as intelligent and competent with my husband's lie (designed to keep me from leaving him) that I was worthless and that no other man would ever want me. He had eroded my self-confidence so subtly and gradually that I hadn't even noticed that he had been tip-toeing around in my brain like a burglar, robbing me of my self-confidence! Now I was reclaiming what was rightfully mine: my confidence and my life. I was granted a $2,500 student loan and used that money to move away from my husband.

Fast-forward to the present day: I am a Ph.D. with four college degrees in psychology, am a bestselling author, have appeared on many national talk shows, have a wonderful relationship, a healthy and attractive figure, and live and write near the water. My current life is an exact replica of the picture that I had in my head! Magic? No. I certainly had to work hard. But, because I was on the "right" track, I was able to realize my highest goals. You can do the same.

Getting on the Right Track

I've found that when we're on the "right track," the world lets us know. Things go smoothly and easily, even if we are working long, hard hours. Doors seem to open. However, when we're on the wrong track—not fulfilling our mission or purpose—the world also gives us plenty of feedback. It's amazing how many things go wrong when the overall picture of our life is off base.

Our appetite for food is usually an accurate reflection of whether we're on the right track or not. When we're living a false life, one that runs counter to our deep, inner vision, we crave food. Instead of healing our life, we mask our problems with the bandage known as food. We act like incarcerated prisoners who, in order to better deal with a miserable state of existence, turn to drugs to numb the reality of life.

Did you know that you have the right to change your life for the better? Did you know that no one else but you is going to give you "permission" to change your life? Did you also know that you can start making those changes *right now*?

The reason why I ask these questions is because when I was living the lie of trying to be an overweight, unhappy, uneducated housewife,

I didn't think I had the right to make any changes. I felt like a prisoner stripped of personal freedom. I was waiting for some "authority figure" to say, "Okay, Doreen, now it's time to take the steps toward leading a happy life." But that was never going to happen because God and I were the only ones who knew my inner dream.

The authority figure, the permission-giver, was deep inside of *me!* I discovered the good news: I had the right to decide how to live my life. I had the right to change my life to fit my inner mission. And so I did—thank God!

Reclaiming the Joy of Marriage

I want to make it clear that by no means am I recommending divorce, separation, or breaking up with a mate as a means of achieving a happy life or significant weight loss. I've worked with many women who falsely blamed their husbands and lovers for being the source of their unhappiness.

One client of mine, Belinda, was convinced that her life would be perfect if she got a divorce. She did so, and was even more miserable! After the divorce, Belinda still had all her old problems because she was the source and originator of them—not her husband. Not only that, but her divorce created financial hardship, the necessity of moving to a smaller apartment, loneliness, and child custody issues.

Divorce isn't a miracle cure for personal dilemmas, including overeating. But when a marriage is unhappy, something has to change. The first step to take when problems develop in a relationship is to seek professional help. Some troubling symptoms may include frequent arguments, tense silences, lack of sexual desire, constantly picking on one another and, of course, physical expressions of anger.

As mentioned previously, though, some people tend to use their marriage as a scapegoat, blaming it for their unhappiness. "If I were in a happy marriage, then *I'd* be happy," or "If it weren't for my husband, I'd have that great job." Instead of taking the frightening steps toward changing their lives for the better, these folks spin their wheels in the mud by blaming their spouses. By remaining in this self-imposed rut, these unhappy people don't have to take responsibility for their own situations.

But guess what? (You can probably predict what I'm about to say.) Your spouse is not responsible for your lack of success, happiness, or nonpursuit of your goals. If you gave away control of your life, that was your choice. But you do have the power to reclaim it.

You see, blaming your partner is a waste of precious time and energy. Focus on clarifying your inner vision, and then affirming that YOU CAN DO IT. The rest will fall into place. If you are married to a healthy person, he will naturally be attracted to the vitality and energy you will begin to exude. He will want to be part of your positive journey, and at that point, you can encourage him to discover the inner vision deep within you.

If, as I was, you are married to a person who feels threatened by your happiness, you may have to consider your options. In fact, let me encourage you right now to use caution when choosing those people whom you allow into your life—whether they be lovers, friends, co-workers, or family members. The people you associate with on a regular basis can have a tremendous uplifting or dispiriting influence on you. Being around negative people who are always echoing "What's the use?" or "Dream on!" or "Life is terrible," or "You're always going to be a loser," has a hypnotic effect. Their negative affirmations interfere with your unconscious belief that you have the right and the strength to succeed.

If, for some reason, you must spend time with negative people (relatives whom you can't always avoid, for instance), try to keep these interactions to a minimum. Arm yourself with affirmations, and slip away from such people now and again (go outside or to the rest room) in order to review these positive thoughts and renew your spirit. If you had to walk into a hospital ward filled with people who had contagious diseases, you'd wear a protective mask and gown, right? It's the same situation here, only the contagious disease is negative thinking.

Your inner self will always guide you, telling you what to do when faced with major decisions such as divorcing a spouse or "divorcing" a negative friend or family member. Spend as much time as you can with your inner voice and vision. If you feel confused or scared, be patient with yourself. The inner voice is clear, but sometimes speaks quietly and is easily drowned out by the noise of negative thinking and fear.

In many cases, overeating is a way to deny the reality of an unhappy marriage. For example, every time my client Patrice stopped overeating, she'd get in arguments with her husband. She wondered if dieting was making her irritable. That can certainly happen, but in Patrice's case, her husband's constant complaining and criticizing was the source of her irritation. As long as Patrice binged on cake and cookies, she was able to numb herself from the pain of her husband's stinging attacks. Without her "food shield," she felt the full force of his verbal slings and arrows.

Patrice's weight-loss efforts were successful only after she directly confronted the issues that were driving her to overeat. Instead of running from her anger, she had to get to its source through marital therapy.

Whenever we feel the urge to overeat, that is our inner voice screaming at us to listen. It needs our attention, because there is something in our life that requires fixing. We overeat to "shut up" the discomfort of having to fix or change the unpleasant areas in our lives. Of course, the pain involved in examining our negative feelings and figuring out their origins is difficult. It's so much easier to grab the quick-fix of food and cover up that annoying inner voice! But, we know too well the consequences of this pseudo-miracle cure: more pain.

In the long run, it is easier to simply sit still and tell your inner voice, "Okay, I'm listening to you. What do you need to tell me?" Here are some ways of tapping into your inner voice and into the answers that lie waiting deep inside you.

❧ Writing ❧

Writing is a wonderful way to have a conversation with yourself. I've employed this method for years, and I still find it useful if I'm feeling upset and confused (which happens to everyone at some time or another). I prefer writing at my computer terminal, because then I can write as quickly as I think. Other people tell me they prefer pen and paper or their typewriter. The medium isn't important, but the act of putting down your thoughts *is*.

The next time you feel upset, I encourage you to start writing without worrying about punctuation, spelling, or grammar. Just let your thoughts and feelings soar, and please don't edit or censor yourself.

❧ Going on a Walk By Yourself ❧

Let the rhythm of your footsteps calm you and help you focus your thoughts. I also find it relaxing to absorb the beautiful colors and sounds of nature. When I'm relaxed, my creative thinking is more active.

❧ Listening to Your Dreams ❧

While we're dreaming, our unconscious mind sifts through the events, problems, and thoughts that we've been involved in during the day. Like a computer, the mind processes all this information and then draws logical conclusions. For example, if a co-worker is plotting to sabotage a project at work, the conscious mind might not acknowledge the danger signals, but the unconscious mind is honest and aware and perceives a lot of important details. In a situation such as this one, you might find yourself having a bad dream where the co-worker is "warning" you about his bad intentions. If you're not in touch with your inner voice these days, your unconscious may try to warn you with an unsettling nightmare. Now, the co-worker may or may not actually be plotting against you; I don't believe that our dreams or unconscious mind can predict the future. However, your unconscious may be acknowledging warning signs that your conscious self is trying to ignore, and the way it relays this information to you is through dreams and nightmares.

A good way to tap into this unconscious well of information is to ask yourself a question right before you fall asleep. For example, you might mentally pose a question such as, "Is this a good time to start looking for a new job?" As you sleep, your unconscious will give you the answers. It might not be a simple answer; for example, your unconscious might reply, "Yes, look for a new job, but don't tell anyone what you're doing," or "First, go to college, then look for a new job."

Dreams and nightmares function as allegories or metaphors. Your unconscious doesn't directly convey information; the answers are implied in symbols. If you get in the habit—as soon as you wake up—of remembering, reviewing, and even writing down your dreams, you'll reap enough information to answer your questions. Interpreting your own dreams is easy; it's just a matter of looking for evidence that supports the answers you already know, deep inside. When you see this proof, it just "clicks" that, yes, here's the answer I'm looking for.

For best results, ask yourself a question three times before falling asleep. Many people find that writing out the question and then putting it under their pillow makes this process more effective.

ૐ Meditating ૐ

Meditating often means nothing more than sitting quietly, clearing your mind of worries and details, and focusing on more important things. Another form of meditation involves repeating a mantra and allowing important information to come into your mind from a higher source. For those of you who have tried either form in the past, you might consider taking it up again. If you haven't meditated before, let me encourage you to make it a part of your life.

You can meditate successfully by yourself or with like-minded folks. I'm such a water baby that I find that my meditating is most effective if I'm surrounded by a lake, the ocean, or even the shower. Water tends to calm me; but for others, a garden, the mountains, or the desert works best.

Many of my clients enjoy converting a little corner or room in their house into a "getaway" place. Everyone needs a private spot, even (especially?) married people, who often share a bedroom and don't have a room to call their very own. This little sanctuary is where you can read, meditate, write, or daydream.

If space is a problem, then consider putting a little desk in a corner, tucked away from distractions such as the television or telephone. This area could reflect your taste and personality by featuring plants and flowers, wall hangings, books, photos, incense, or whatever makes you feel happy and content.

Setting up this private place is just one more way of being good to yourself, a way to replace your pounds of pain with health and joy!

"STOP THE WORLD, I WANT TO GET OFF!": STRESS AND STRESS EATING

"Suffering ceases to be suffering in some way at the moment it finds a meaning."
—Viktor Frankl, psychiatrist who survived Nazi concentration camp and wrote about his experiences in *Man's Search for Meaning*

ABUSE SURVIVORS who don't deal with their closeted anger and self-blame often enter emotionally abusive adulthood situations at work or in their love lives. These people may pride themselves on being exceptionally strong and able to withstand tremendous adversity, but the price of bearing this high threshold of pain is enormous.

A person who grows up in a warm, loving environment devoid of neglect or abuse won't stand for abuse as an adult. If she finds her professional environment unbearable, she looks for other work. Childhood abuse survivors who attempt to endure adulthood abuse (in a marriage or job, for example) will also display symptoms of discontent, such as weight gain and health problems. But the abuse survivor often blocks out awareness of this feedback from her body. She denies it and downplays its severity.

You see, there is a difference between a stressful situation and an abusive situation. Stress, like abuse, commonly leads to overeating, but stress is unavoidable, while abuse is. Stress doesn't mean that your personal rights are being violated, but abuse does. Stressful situations can actually increase your self-esteem and strength, while abuse tears you down.

To combat stress eating, you need to take personal measures and make personal changes, while to combat abuse, you need to completely distance yourself from the perpetrator of the abuse.

The Co-ed's Weight Gain

If you were raised in a warm, nurturing family, you may have been shielded from stress until early adulthood. That sudden shock of diving into the cold water of life often catches the young adult unprepared for the challenges involved in independent living. And that initial brush with stress can also mean an encounter with out-of-control eating and weight gain.

I've counseled a number of women who complained that they never had a weight problem until they went away to college. This happened to Grace when she turned 18 and left home to attend a prestigious university 150 miles away. She'd had to work hard to be accepted to the competitive college, and she was determined to be at the head of the class, as she had been in high school.

To her dismay, Grace soon discovered that she'd gone from being the big fish in a small pond, to a small fish in a big pond. "College was so much harder than I expected!" she remembers. "I had to study all the time just to keep a *B* average." In high school, she'd breezed through her courses.

Grace's academic pressures were compounded by her loneliness. She missed her parents, her sister, her boyfriend, and her other friends. She found it difficult to socialize with the seemingly sophisticated college kids, and with her intense studying schedule, she had little time for leisure or recreation.

All this stress triggered an enormous appetite for food that Grace had never experienced before. The dorm food was high-fat: pizzas, cheeseburgers, french fries, and the like. It tasted delicious to Grace's empty stomach and soul. She ate more than she had before, and exercised much less than she had previously. These two factors added up to 25 extra pounds on her 5'5" frame. To worsen the situation, she now felt fat, which further added to her shyness.

Clearly, Grace wasn't being abused. She'd come from a loving family and had never acted out addictively before. We did find a history of alcoholism in parts of Grace's family (not her parents), so she may have had some genetic predisposition to binging on food or alcohol, but until people with this proclivity are faced with abuse or undue stress, this dormant tendency may not be triggered. In Grace's case, she met with overwhelming stress for the first time at age 18. And without any outlet for it—such as emotional support or exercise —she began acting out addictively to ease her pain.

"I Can't Stand My Job!"

I've worked with people who were experiencing significant job stress, as well as those in abusive employment settings. Here are their stories, to further illustrate the difference between job stress and job abuse:

> — During the Christmas season, Mandy and her coworkers were always asked to work overtime to meet increased customer demand. Since it was so exhausting and stressful to deal with the crowds for 10 to 12 hours a day, and because she had little time for exercise, Mandy's incessant nibbling on holiday sweets caused her to gain 10 or more pounds. This is an example of stress eating.

> — Paulette's boss also wanted his employees to meet increased orders occurring during Christmas rush. Unlike Mandy's situation, however, Paulette's supervisor would make demands on his employees in an abusive fashion. He'd scream at his workers to work faster, often using demeaning and profane language, and he'd even call them at home to ask them ridiculous questions. Despite Paulette's deeply held religious beliefs, her boss insisted that she

work on Sundays, preventing her from attending church, and he threatened to fire her if she didn't adhere to his every command. Paulette was so upset by this situation that she started to binge on food, but the weight that she gained only made her feel worse.

— Marcia worked for a defense contractor. During the 1980s, thousands of workers had been hired to fulfill the demands created by the company's lucrative military contracts. But after the end of the cold war, the company's production practically ceased. Marcia knew that 3,500 workers were due to be laid off during the coming two years, so every morning, she'd wake up wondering: "Is this the day I lose my job?" She witnessed her co-workers being laid off, one by one, and as the stress of waiting for her fate to be determined became unbearable, she soon began eating huge lunches and fattening snacks. Another example of stress eating.

— Another stress eater was Joel, a policeman for five years. The constant danger inherent in his profession caused him to feel tense on a regular basis, and he'd wind down at night with potato chips, popcorn, pretzels, and other unhealthful foods.

— Kelly's stress stemmed from being in a job that was totally unsuited to her personality. She was an energetic, creative person who enjoyed working on independent projects. So why was she employed as an insurance claims adjuster? It had been the first job she had been offered out of college, and she'd snapped it up. Now, Kelly was miserable, feeling smothered by the enormous paperwork and the huge and impersonal insurance system, and she overate to try to assuage her discontent.

When I asked her why she didn't seek different work,

I was surprised at her reply: "In only 14 years, I can re-tire." I don't know about you, but to me, 14 years is an awfully long time to be miserable. Since it was impracti-cal for Kelly to quit her job in the uncertain economy, we worked on ways to improve her situation on a daily basis. Instead of concentrating on the negative aspects of her job, Kelly learned to focus on those areas that were somewhat creative and satisfying, such as calming people and help-ing them recover from losses. As her attitude improved, she also found that her eating habits returned to normal.

As was the case with Kelly, most people deal with job stress by mak-ing changes in their attitudes or work environment. If you have an abu-sive boss or co-worker, however, the problem needs to be dealt with head-on. Ignoring abuse doesn't work. Removing yourself from the abusive situation is the only solution, either by transferring to another department, finding another job, or taking steps to have the abusive person punished or removed. Neither step is easy. And with economic uncertainty, most of us are reluctant to rock the boat. But if an abu-sive job situation is negatively affecting your weight and other areas of your health, do you have any choice but to listen to your body and confront the problem?

Of course, obesity results in additional pain. Unfortunately, many people act cruel toward those who are different from the norm, and obese people are often on the receiving end of incredible insensitiv-ity, directed toward them by their fellow human beings. A person who would never poke fun at a member of a racial minority or a disabled person may not even hesitate to call a very overweight person "Fatso" or some other disparaging epithet.

A Harvard University study conducted from 1981 to 1988 found that overweight women were 20 percent less likely to be married, were not as educated, and earned an average of $6,710 less a year than thin-ner women. Overweight men were 11 percent less likely to be mar-ried and earned about $3,000 less a year than thinner men. It can be argued that being single is not necessarily a problem. After all, some people prefer this state. However, I believe that many grossly over-weight people have suffered sexual traumas that make them avoid, or even sabotage, long-term relationships and marriage.

Clearly, though, a number of well-constructed studies have pointed to employment discrimination toward overweight people. This is just one objective indicator of what every overweight person knows too well: Society blames you, even hates you, if you're fat.

I know from first-hand experience that when I would gain just a little weight—say, 20 pounds—people would treat me differently. Men would no longer open doors for me or ask me out on dates. I became invisible.

This mistreatment leads to more isolation, loneliness, and other feel-ings that trigger eating binges. If you're depressed because you're be-ing teased and taunted, how are you going to ease your pain? With food, of course. If you're angry because nothing in your closet fits on your ever-growing body, how are you going to calm down? By eat-ing, naturally.

The Pain of Loss and Grieving

Losing a loved one is never easy. The grieving triggered by a sig-nificant loss is intermixed with other painful feelings such as: Was it my fault? Could I have prevented this somehow? Why did this have to happen? How can I go on?

The process of grieving was studied by noted author Elisabeth Kübler-Ross, who wrote that grief often involves shock and disbelief, followed by attempts to "bargain" with God over the loss ("I'll go to church every Sunday if only you allow her to live"). Next, the bereaved person feels anger and betrayal, either directed toward her-self, toward God, toward the situation, or toward the person who passed away. After the anger stage, grieving moves into the depres-sion phase—what we usually think of as mourning.

Gradually, the pain subsides and, in most cases, after about six or nine months there is an acceptance of the loss, and the grieving per-son goes on with her life.

Many times, though, a person gets "stuck" in one of the stages of grief. Anger and depression are the most common stopping points for people who haven't come to terms with a loss. And those who are stuck in one of these stages are likely to overeat. My clients who have overindulged in food because of unresolved grief have experienced many different types of losses—not all of which were related to someone's death:

— Suzanne witnessed her mother having a heart attack, and her efforts to save her were futile.

— Jim lost his right hand in an industrial accident.

— Edith's father had shot her pet dog for committing the crime of digging up the family vegetable garden. Her grief involved unresolved anger toward her father, as well as grief over the loss of her best friend, the dog. Pet loss triggers a lot of unresolved grief because many people don't openly mourn for animals—they're afraid that people will think it's silly. But, our relationships with beloved animals are often as close as they are with humans.

— Monica's emotional pain stemmed from her grandmother's death three years before. Her grandmother had been her role model, confidante, and best friend, and she was having trouble dealing with her feelings of grief, even though quite a bit of time had elapsed since the death.

— Ruby had lost custody of her little girl, and she described the emotional pain as being similar to a death. (I wrote about the grieving connected to lost and shared custody—for fathers, mothers, and grandparents—in my first book, *My Kids Don't Live with Me Anymore: Coping with the Custody Crisis.*)

— Phyllis's husband had left her two years before, and she still mourned the loss of her "ideal marriage" dream. Although the marriage had never been harmonious, Phyllis hung on to the resentment and anger that she experienced as a result of her husband's sudden departure.

— Nicki had worked 12 years for the same company and always believed that her job was secure, even when she found out that a mass layoff was in the works. So, when she was given a pink slip in her paycheck, she felt as if she'd been betrayed. Her grief was compounded by the losses attached to her new financial problems: She had to move from the home she had resided in for 20 years into a cheaper apartment, and she had to trade in her pride-and-joy red sports car for a basic sedan.

The Grief Aspect of Dieting

The most difficult loss, for compulsive overeaters, is giving up their very close companion and comforting friend—food. Relinquishing chocolate ice cream, cheeseburgers, or whatever food got them through life's difficult moments feels like the death of a loved one.

I've examined this aspect of weight loss extensively and have discovered that it's very important to acknowledge the loss of food in one's life. The stages of grieving in this regard are exactly like those connected to other types of losses. During the shock phase, you blindly agree to do anything to lose weight—buy expensive gym memberships, sign up with weight-reducing organizations and, of course, swear off overeating.

The anger phase of grieving is two-fold: First, the dieter struggles with questions such as: "Why me? Why do I gain weight so easily? How could I have let myself get so fat? Why can't I be like my husband, who can eat anything and never gain a pound?" Second, all the pent-up anger she's been holding in—and repressing with eating binges—comes rushing to the surface. Many people rationalize that the irritability that they feel at this stage is from dieting, and they give themselves an excuse to go off their diet at this point.

The third stage of grief involves "bargaining," which means trying to negotiate with yourself, the universe, or God. The bargaining dieter tries to stretch the laws concerning physics, digestion, calorie-burning, and metabolism, to fit her own needs. For example, she may tell herself, "It's okay for me to eat a lot at Sunday brunch because tomorrow morning I'm joining the gym," or "I'll have a second helping of dinner, and then skip breakfast tomorrow."

After bargaining comes depression. The dieter reaches a behavioral fork in the road at this stage. She may say, "What's the use? I'll always be fat!" and abandon any attempt toward achieving a healthful lifestyle. Or, she may continue her diet and overindulge in destructive behavior involving drugs, alcohol, shopping, promiscuity, or smoking in order to combat the depression.

Much depression is rooted in anger that is turned inward. The result is self-blame or "Shame"—the *S* in the F.A.T.S. feelings leading to overeating. Food has many chemicals, textures, and properties that deliver antidepressant effects. That's why food is so seductive to the depressed person. (Chapter 10 delves into this topic and offers suggestions for bypassing shame-based eating.)

The final stage of grief is acceptance. The healthy dieter who has successfully worked through the stages of grieving and has diligently adhered to a balanced nutrition program has realized the true meaning of this concept. *Acceptance* means acknowledging that eating healthfully is a way of life and not just something you do as a quick-fix. She accepts the reality of her body's physics: If she eats too much, she gains weight. If she eats moderately and exercises, she loses weight and tones her muscles.

Acceptance means that you understand and internalize these realities. To accept means to face something head-on and to take responsibility for your actions. It doesn't mean wallowing in questions of "Why?" It means figuring out how to make the best of any particular situation.

Post-Traumatic Eating

Stress resulting from an unexpected trauma can also trigger over-eating. After the 1994 Los Angeles earthquake, *Los Angeles Times* columnist Robin Abcarian reported on how utterly unnerving it was to experience the sudden buckling of the ground. Abcarian wrote that she and her friends had replaced their normally low-calorie diets with high-fat, high-bulk, and high-carbohydrate foods. The muffins, bacon, cheeseburgers, and the like were filling and comforting, calming jittery nerves fueled by too many aftershocks.

My client, Shirley, reacted in a similar way to a sudden trauma. One night while driving home from a class, a loud stomach-churning thud signaled that her car had made impact with something. She stopped the car and realized, to her horror, that she had accidentally hit a bicyclist.

Another driver called an ambulance. Shirley was so busy attending to the fallen victim that she didn't even notice that her nose had been broken when her face had hit the steering wheel. Unfortunately, the bicyclist died the next day, and Shirley started psychotherapy two weeks later.

With her conscience eating away at *her*, Shirley was eating away at food to compensate. Her heart hurt, her nose ached, and her body felt painfully swollen by the ten pounds she'd put on so quickly. She was haunted by painful memories of the accident, and was barely able to sleep due to recurring nightmares.

Post-traumatic stress disorder is a coping mechanism. The body throws a switch in response to sudden and overwhelming fear, a switch that alters the behavior and emotions. Insecurity, obtrusive thoughts, worry, and nightmares cloud the lives of trauma survivors, and they turn to food to placate these feelings.

In subsequent chapters, I'll discuss some of the biological reasons why we overeat in response to trauma and stress. You'll also read about ways to replace overeating with healthier, more effective, coping measures.

Picking on Yourself

Sometimes abuse is self-inflicted, as opposed to being perpetrated by another party. Many of my clients with low self-esteem didn't feel that they deserved good. They denied themselves basic necessities, behaving like stingy parents neglecting their own selves.

— Although Mindy and her husband were financially secure, she wouldn't spend much money on herself. She always bought her children and husband top-quality shoes, clothes, and undergarments. Yet, Mindy dressed in dime-store housedresses and cheap vinyl shoes. I asked about the condition of her bras, panties, and socks, and Mindy reluctantly admitted that they were worn, faded, and ill-fitting. I literally had to give Mindy an "assignment" to purchase new clothes for herself. The transformation in her self-esteem was immediately apparent.

— Judy had a self-destructive habit bordering on obsessive-compulsive behavior: she constantly picked at her face. She'd squeeze pimples and blackheads and gouge chin hairs with her tweezers until her face was bleeding. Judy's complexion was always rough due to this mishandling, and she told me that her facial skin often hurt.

— Dana's life would have been so much easier if she had made a point of maintaining her car. Instead, she waited for things to break. As a result, she risked serious injury as a result of blown tires and gaskets and near-failing brakes, and she was perpetually late.

— Jeannie's overeating was clearly an act of self-abuse. She desperately wanted to lose the extra 80 pounds she carried, yet believed she wasn't capable of achieving her goal.

he felt totally incompetent and blamed herself for many things that she had no control over. To punish herself for "being bad," she'd stuff herself with food until she felt nauseated by the pressure in her stomach.

Clearly, self-abuse can be deadly. Many of the sexually abused clients I've worked with had attempted suicide. Many had slashed their wrists and other parts of their bodies. According to Wallace (1993), a recent survey in *Who's Who Among American High School Students* recently reported that 20 percent of the nation's brightest female students said they had been sexually assaulted by someone they knew. Of those who had been sexually assaulted, 56 had experienced suicidal thoughts, and 17 percent had actually attempted suicide.

Now, although not as dangerous as the examples mentioned above, people experiencing low-level cumulative stress (that stems from a lot of little things) can eat away at a person after a while, too. However, it's important to note that easing this type of stress can be of great benefit to someone's overall life. Here are some examples of stress situations that were fairly easily overcome.

— Henrietta was disorganized and had to hunt for her keys and purse every morning, as well as pens, scissors, and other basics. So, she made a point of placing those items that she would need near the door the night before.

— Every day Margaret struggled with a garage door opener that almost slammed on her car as she was backing out her car. A call to a handyman solved a problem that had been nagging at her for months.

— Vicki kept breaking her fingernails on the rusty combination lock she used at her gym. When she finally replaced the lock for a mere five dollars, she eased that annoyance.

— Melissa was chronically late returning library books and was always shelling out 10, 12, or 15 dollars in late fees. Part of the problem was that the library was 10 miles away from her office and home. Melissa decided it was more economical, and less stressful, to purchase her reading material instead of borrowing it.

— Anita hadn't balanced her checkbook in over a year, so she had no idea how much available money she actually had available to spend. She bounced checks often, and the overdraft charges of $15 were eating away at her meager savings. So, she decided to open up a new account and keep careful records of her assets and debits.

— Leigh's finances were also out of control, but her situation stemmed from excessive credit card charging. Her "cure" was to tear up her cards and pay off her balances as quickly as possible.

Self-Imposed Stress and Self-Esteem

All of the clients cited in the examples above had suffered from low self-esteem before they inflicted their self-imposed abuse. But clearly, by not taking care of themselves, their self-esteem had little chance of improving.

In the case of someone being disorganized, this habit is one that can be deeply ingrained from the time of childhood. Other times, the person becomes increasingly used to denying herself anything good or valuable.

I especially see this trait when I watch the buying habits of these women. No matter what, they never buy anything for themselves unless it's on sale. It doesn't matter if there are two identical items, priced exactly the same. If one has a price tag that says it's marked down, that's the one they'll buy. They don't feel that they deserve, or have the right to possess, a full-priced item.

Sometimes, my clients are afraid to tell their husbands they've purchased something. Diana would hang her clothing purchases in the depths of her closet for at least two months before wearing them. Then, if her husband noticed her wearing a new dress or blouse, she could truthfully say that she'd had it for "months."

This type of sneaking also eats away at self-esteem.

Many of my clients also implied that they didn't think they deserved to take good care of themselves until they'd lost weight. This is backwards, I'd explain to them. First, you take good care of yourself, then your self-esteem goes up. When your self-esteem goes up, your appetite and weight go down.

You must take good care of yourself even if you don't believe that you deserve it. "Act" as if you have high self-esteem. Pretend that you are someone you admire, such as a famous movie star. Pretend that you are a thin person. Then act the way that you envision that person acting. Your self-esteem will catch up to your self-loving behavior.

Deep inside, your inner child will be happy that you are taking good care of her. She'll think, "Gee, I must be a special little girl to deserve such good treatment." And when the little girl inside of you feels good about herself, it's reflected in the way that *you* feel about yourself.

Consider this: You like to be around people who treat you well, don't you? People who say nice things to you and who consider your needs and feelings? And, conversely, wouldn't you prefer to avoid people who say negative things to you and who are selfish? Well, you can have the same relationship priorities with your own self. If you are nice to yourself, you'll be happier and more comfortable. If you neglect yourself, you'll feel unloved and lonely.

The point to remember is: First, be good to yourself. *Then* you'll lose weight.

PLAYING DOCTOR
ISN'T CHILD'S PLAY

"I have never begun any important venture for which I felt adequately prepared."
—Dr. Sheldon Kopp, author of *Raise Your Right Hand Against Fear!*

STEPHANIE, a 33-year-old legal secretary, was crying as she sat in my office. "My husband says our sex life isn't good enough for him," she said, blinking her tear-stained blue eyes. "I know what the problem is. I know it's because I'm too fat!" She sobbed uncontrollably into her tissue, repeating how unattractive she felt, complaining that her overweight body was the cause of her unhappiness. The truth, of course, was the reverse: Her unhappiness precipitated the fat on her body.

I requested that she bring Raymond, her husband, in with her for the next therapy session. She did so, and although Raymond seemed uncomfortable at first, after listening to Stephanie for a while, he poured his heart out in an impassioned manner.

"Stephanie, your body has nothing to do with our problems!" he told her emphatically. "I wouldn't mind if you'd lose some weight, but the main problem is you never want sex. And when we finally do make love, you seem to be completely turned off. It's like your body's there, but your heart's not into it at all. How am I supposed to be turned on if you're not turned on, too?"

Stephanie looked shocked by her husband's protestations. She almost couldn't believe that it wasn't her soft, billowy body that was the principal problem in the bedroom, and that Raymond wasn't turned off by her cellulite.

Once Stephanie understood Raymond's position—that he wanted his wife to fully participate in their sex life—the couple was on the road to healing. I worked with them with respect to communicating their desires and fears within the relationship, and we also discussed ways of heightening sexual pleasure for both of them.

I worked particularly hard with Stephanie in an effort to discover the root of her inability to *enjoy* making love. It turned out that Stephanie needed to give herself permission to relax and enjoy sex. Her early experiences, we discovered, had taught Stephanie that sex was dirty and wrong.

At the time of her first sexual experience, Stephanie was five years old, a cute wide-eyed brunette with a big smile. Stephanie's big brother, Bob, had taken her to a neighbor's house on one of those Saturday mornings when time stretches out endlessly in front of children. The neighbor children's parents were gone for the day, leaving their three sons home alone. That also meant that Stephanie was alone in a house with four preadolescent males—a combustible situation.

As if they had planned it, one of the neighbor boys asked Bob to practice hoopshots in the backyard with him. This left Stephanie alone with the other two boys, Tony and David, who asked her if she wanted to "play doctor." The little girl, not knowing any better, said okay. She would be the patient, the boys said, and they would be the two doctors.

"First, you take off all your clothes," said Tony. Stephanie complied, too young to be controlled by modesty impulses. Once she was naked, Tony told her to lie on the bed. "Okay, pretend you're really sick, and we'll take care of you."

The boys—overwhelmed by curiosity and never before having seen a naked girl—ran their hands all over her body. They paid very close attention to Stephanie's genitals, spreading her legs and exploring her labia and vaginal opening. Stephanie was eager to comply and didn't protest, except when David stuck his finger into her vagina.

"Ouch!" she yelped, "You're hurting me!"

"Just relax," David forcefully told her. "Remember, we're doctors and we have to do this."

Stephanie closed her eyes tightly and put her hands flat against her hips to brace against the pain. Tears rolled down her eyes as Tony and David continued exploring her genitals.

''Hey, what are you doing!?" The bedroom door slammed open as Bob and his friend returned from playing basketball. Bob glared at Tony and David, and their brother was yelling at the two younger boys.

"Get dressed. Let's get out of here, Steph!" Bob ordered his little sister. She struggled to pull up her little pants and grimaced at the pain when the fabric touched her tender genitals. Stephanie walked gingerly downstairs as Bob urged her to exit quickly.

Bob and Stephanie told their parents everything that had happened, expecting the adults to intervene by admonishing the neighbors. Instead, Bob and Stephanie were both spanked—hard—for their "foolishness." Confused and humiliated, Stephanie's views on sexuality had just been formed.

So it was no wonder that Stephanie avoided having sex. She had always associated the act with pain, exploitation, and punishment.

The Myth of Playing Doctor

Many "child care experts" dismiss childhood sexual exploration as harmless, since sexual curiosity is normal and natural. While curiosity *is* natural to children, and this curiosity often leads to the exploration of male/female differences, "playing doctor" is not a harmless avenue. Too many boys and girls, such as Stephanie, are victimized at the hands of older children. David and Tony ignored the little girl's cries and protestations and used her body to satisfy themselves. They crossed the line into abuse because they got carried away and didn't care about Stephanie.

Harmless sexual exploration does exist, of course. Prepubescent boys look at their own genitals and masturbate. Little girls marvel at the sensations of their labia and clitoris touching a bicycle seat or a horse's back. And same-sex exploration is extremely common among both sexes. In fact, I've had a number of clients come to terms with fears that they were homosexual, when all they had been doing as children was exploring their newly discovered sexuality.

For example, Kathleen and her four close girlhood friends had touched each other's naked breasts and labia during slumber parties. For years, Kathleen kept this a closely guarded secret, feeling that she'd committed some horrible "crime." When she learned, in therapy, that her experience was fairly common among young people, she was greatly relieved.

Jerry had similar fears about the mutual masturbation sessions he and his best friend, Andy, had engaged in during one summer vacation. They'd taken turns holding each other's penis and "jerking each other off" until ejaculating. At the time, it had been a powerful sexual experience that they both enjoyed immensely and laughed about. Over the years, though—especially since his relationships with women weren't working very well—Jerry harbored secret fears that he might be gay. Like Kathleen, Jerry was comforted by the fact that his childhood experiences were actually quite common.

The line between normal sexual exploration and sexual abuse is crossed as soon as one person is not a voluntary participant. The child who is pressured, coerced, tricked, forced, or manipulated is the one who suffers the emotional consequences of being an abuse survivor. It is those emotions, not the actual physical sexual act, that cause the harm and confusion.

That is why "playing doctor" can be just as emotionally detrimental to children as full-on intercourse. The physical manifestation of sexual abuse can take any form, but if the child is flooded with feelings too powerful to handle or understand, the child is emotionally injured.

The Pound/Pain Link

Today, many people have become cognizant of the emotional reasons behind overeating. We overeat because of stress, anger, fatigue, depression, loneliness, and insecurity. However, abuse survivors overeat without conscious awareness that they have any choice over eating. Abuse survivors, in other words, feel *compelled* to overeat. They literally eat like there is no tomorrow because, for the abused, "tomorrow" is an abstract concept. The past, instead, rules their lives.

Playing doctor in abusive ways makes children particularly ripe for eating disorders. Becky, for example, was six years old when her older stepbrother, Michael, locked her in the bathroom and convinced her to take a shower with him. He seductively soaped Becky's body and spent way too much time lathering her genitals with his hands.

Becky was frightened. She was afraid that Michael would reject her if she protested. She was afraid that her parents would disapprove—or worse. Becky was also fearful because the situation just felt wrong. Yet, at the same time, she was aware of pleasurable sensations induced by the warm, soapy water and the effect of Michael's fingers stroking her vaginal opening.

But her pleasure was short-lived when, after the shower, Michael painfully gripped Becky's shoulders, shook her hard, and warned in a menacing voice, "Don't you ever tell Mom and Dad we took a shower together. If you do, they'll have a big fight and probably get a divorce. And it will be all *your* fault!"

Becky, at age six, had just learned that pleasure and fear were interrelated. This process, whereby humans and animals can be changed after one powerful emotional experience, is called "one-trial learning." For example, if a balloon pops loudly near your dog, he may, from that point onward, react with fear to the sound of balloons. Someone who eats a bad piece of fish and gets violently ill may feel nauseated by the smell of cooking fish, even for years after the original experience occurred.

In Becky's case, she experienced two powerful sensations simultaneously—sexual arousal and intense fear—and she linked the two together. As Becky grew up, her relationships with boys were affected by this one-trial learning experience. When she was 14 and kissed a boy for the first time, the sexual arousal she felt scared her to the point that she avoided this boy forever after. When she got married, sex was something that Becky avoided, as well.

Our sexuality is also deeply linked to our self-image. We all have private, inner lives and feelings about who we are, deep inside ourselves. Our sexuality is a bridge between our inner, private selves and our public selves. Sex is something deeply personal, yet it also something we share with certain other people.

Our first sexual experiences often set the tone for how we view the other private parts of ourselves. If we have a negative initial sexual experience—as Becky did—we internalize this negativity and apply those feelings of fear, shame, and anger to ourselves. Becky had every right to be furious with her stepbrother, but she was too young to know who was truly responsible for their ill-advised shower. Before the age of ten, children see themselves as the center of the universe—everything revolves around them. So, naturally, this unfortunate shower experience must have been Becky's fault.

Becky felt deep fear and insecurity after her experience in the shower, but what she really felt was defective. She was intensely ashamed by her feelings of sexual arousal, and she was convinced that she was the only person who had ever had those sensations. She had nightmares about adults touching her genitals, and during those dreams, Becky was sexually aroused. Then she'd wake up in a cold sweat. Normally, Becky would cry out to her mother after a nightmare, but now she was too frightened to tell anyone about her bad dreams.

Instead, Becky turned to food for solace. She was especially fond of peanut butter and jelly sandwiches, which comforted her when she did her homework alone in her room at night. The extra-crunchy peanut butter and crisp toasted bread helped ease the fear and anxiety that were buried so deeply below the surface that Becky actually began to think it was normal to feel afraid and insecure. As long as she was eating, Becky felt okay about herself.

While Becky was never obese as an adult, she constantly carried 25 extra pounds on her 5'5" body. The sandwiches kept Becky's sexual arousal level, fears, and insecurities out of conscious awareness. She also avoided attracting much male sexual attention by staying slightly plump and then by dressing unattractively. Anytime a man looked her way, Becky would catch her breath and feel flushed with mild anxiety.

Healing the Pound/Pain Link

Becky, as well as other "playing doctor" survivors, turned to food out of necessity, since little girls have few emotional anesthetics available to them. If the trauma had occurred during adulthood, Becky could have chosen from adult-type outlets, some healthy some not. She could have shopped, jogged, seen a therapist, gotten drunk, smoked pot, argued with her husband, yelled at her children, driven her car fast, written in her journal, or called her best friend. But all Becky had, at age six, was food. She was too ashamed to talk to her mother about her experiences, and she certainly couldn't talk to her stepbrother. She didn't know about organized forms of physical exercise, and she was too young to go shopping or call someone. So she ate.

Growing up, Becky repressed the memories of that unpleasant shower experience. Occasionally, the incident would pop into her mind, but she would immediately dismiss it as something minor and insignificant. When she started therapy as an adult, Becky told the therapist she'd had a "perfect childhood with no abuse at all." Becky had even convinced herself that the shower incident was unimportant in the shaping of her self-image.

As I've worked with abuse survivors over the years, I've seen this type of scenario again and again. The original hurtful situation is a faint, recurring memory disregarded as inconsequential. So, in light of the information that has been presented up to this point, here's the first step in breaking the pound/pain link:

our history.

a memory resurfaces once or twice a month, that memory is trying to tell you something. Think of the memory as a teacher who has something for you to learn. Though it may be frightening or painful to learn that teacher's lesson, in the long run, life will be calmer and make more sense. In other words, it is worth taking the time and trouble to listen to your inner teacher.

Is there a faint, distant memory that pops up in your mind periodically? I'm not asking you to create one, but instead, be aware of what's already there. Whenever I ask a client this question, they quickly downplay the importance of any recurring memory they may have. That tendency stems from the fact that the person has lived with the memory for a long time, and it has been integrated into her internal landscape. It is a familiar scene, and this familiarity causes it to be dismissed as ordinary and insignificant.

However, as soon as the recurring memory is discussed in therapy, the client instantly recognizes the powerful emotions that still lie behind the memory. And that takes us to Step 2 in your healing process.

2. *Write a one- or two-sentence description of your memory.*

At this point, you needn't elaborate on your original hurtful situation. You just need to recategorize it, from a seemingly fictitious and faded memory, to a significant piece of your personal history. In other words, you need to make the memory real.

If you write down a very brief description of your memory, it will stop haunting you. Even if you're not precisely sure what happened, and even if you're not entirely certain that it actually occurred, write down the memory. We're not going to make a big deal out of this memory or turn it into something more than it was. We're simply going to listen to it.

3. Be aware of the emotions accompanying the memory.

As you write down the memory, pay attention to any emotional reactions you may have. Do you feel nervous, tense, or anxious at all? Is your jaw tight, or your fists clenched? Is your heart pounding? Do you feel lightheaded or dizzy? Or do you have doubts about the credibility of the memory and wonder whether writing it down might be opening a "can of worms"? These are emotions you can expect to feel when the recurring memory is nailed down on paper.

Another reaction might be your desire to put this book down for a while to avoid dealing with this subject. Other people might find that their appetite for food increases as they recall these memories, with the added frustration that they are temporarily overeating while reading this book. But, in the long run, by becoming more aware of how normal these reactions are, you can progress on your path toward serenity and a normal body weight.

You see, your food cravings and increased appetite are teachers in the same respect that your recurring memory is a teacher. There are important lessons inherent in these sensations, and until the lessons are digested, the teachers won't go away. Instead of getting angry at yourself for eating all the time, this could be the point where you begin to take a different approach to your overactive appetite. Instead of fighting with your appetite or being controlled by it, you might discover why it is so large to begin with.

The first part of healing occurs in the mind. The second part occurs in the heart. The third and final part of healing occurs in the stomach. The first step is to achieve an intellectual understanding of the painful situations triggering overeating. Then, the next step is to acknowledge and release the powerful emotions attached to the situations. When that happens, the stomach reacts by triggering the return to a normal appetite for food. Our appetite will no longer need our attention because we will have learned its lessons. We won't *need* to be hungry anymore.

Keep going!

67

SUBTLE AND NOT-SO-SUBTLE
FORMS OF ABUSE

"Believe that life is worth living, and your belief
will help create that fact."
    —William James, psychologist/philosopher

A STRANGELY SAD occurrence often happens during early adolescence. Young girls' self-esteem levels drop markedly, at about the same time that their breasts and sexuality begin to develop. As far as I'm concerned, there is a direct cause-and-effect relationship between these two milestones—that is, girls' emerging sexual attractiveness and their lowered self-esteem.

When males first pay sexual attention to a young girl, it can be both confusing and frightening. Parents and teachers rarely prepare an adolescent or pre-adolescent for this turn of events, and girls often have no idea how to react to this new situation.

I remember the first time a man whistled at me. I was riding my Stingray bicycle at age 12. My breasts had just begun to develop—no more than little mounds that wouldn't fit in the teeniest training bra—but breasts, nonetheless. I was a little girl with an emerging woman's body and very little awareness of the complexity of male/female relationships.

When I heard the unmistakable wolf whistle, I turned my head to see who was being whistled at. I expected to see, well, a woman. Instead, I saw a man driving a Ford Mustang with his head hanging out the window and his eyes on *me*. Why would a man whistle at me, a little girl of average attractiveness, I remember thinking. There must be some mistake. But after that first time, it kept happening. Men and boys were noticing me, and I didn't know how to handle it.

Why didn't I talk to my mother about this new development in my life? Looking back, I guess that the attention I received from men at that time really didn't affect me that much. Also, the onset of the wolf whistles and other indicators of male appreciation happened so gradually that eventually I guess I got used to it.

But, in retrospect, it really is an awkward time in a girl's life, to say the least. On the one hand, females enjoy the audible and visible signs of male approval. On the other hand, the attention can be embarrassing, for many young girls don't know how to react to it. Do we smile, or does this encourage the man? Do we ignore him, or does this make us look stuck-up? Do we flip the man the bird, or does this make us look bitchy?

Isn't it complicated being a woman?

The type of harmless flirting mentioned above is fairly innocent in nature, with the most serious result being embarrassment on the part of the female recipient. And, in some cases, flirting can be pleasant and even uplifting, if the man involved is skillful and sincere. The best "pick-up line" I ever received was when a man came up to me at the grocery store and gushed, "I can't *believe* there's no wedding ring on that finger of yours!" Harmless stuff, that type of flirting.

However, flirting crosses the line into abuse when one of the following situations occurs:

1. There is psychological sexual abuse—that is, when an "inappropriate" adult—such as your parent, sibling, boss, uncle, doctor, and so on—relates to you in a sexual manner.

2. Put-downs are implicit in the flirting. For example, if someone implies that you are "cheap," "easy," promiscuous, or slutty, that does not constitute simple flirtation but, rather, a form of abuse.

3. Inappropriate sexual touching is involved.

We'll explore all three situations in this chapter, as well as come to understand how they are linked to overeating. Later on in the book, we'll discuss ways to heal this pound/pain link so that your appetite and body weight can both return to normal.

Psychological Sexual Abuse

I've counseled numerous clients who were scarred—not by physical sexual assaults—but by psychological ones. And, of the two, the psychological sexual abuse cases often make the most impact. The subtle, almost intangible nature of this form of abuse leaves the victim feeling like she's trying to hold onto a cloud or a mirage. She knows there's something there, but she can't quite put her finger on it.

Don't get me wrong. Victims of rape or incest have an enormous amount of traumatic baggage to contend with, as will be amplified upon in subsequent chapters. But survivors of psychological sexual abuse tend to struggle with the troubling notion that, "Well, nothing that bad really happened to me." They constantly deny and dismiss their painful memories.

Psychological sexual abuse takes on many forms. Some of the stories that follow—as experienced by my own clients over the years—illustrate the many different ways in which this life-altering situation can manifest itself.

— Brenda grew up in a house where sexually explicit material was openly displayed. Everything from soft-core pornographic magazines to X-rated books and sex paraphernalia catalogs were strewn on the living room coffee table. Brenda would browse through these publications when her parents weren't around, and although she didn't fully understand what she was looking at, this material did shape her feelings with respect to how a woman was supposed to look and behave. The situation wasn't helped by the fact that Brenda would crouch by the staircase at night, looking on in awe as her parents watched X-rated movies.

As an adult, Brenda could never shake the deep-seated

feeling that sex was dirty, a way of thinking that interfered with her marital relationship. She seesawed between voraciously craving food and struggling to achieve the body dimensions of a magazine centerfold—two desires that manifested themselves in a severe case of bulimia.

— Teresa's father and stepmother thought they were doing her a favor by being very open about matters of a sexual nature. Both adults walked around the house naked, and Teresa was encouraged to shower with them. Not only that, but Teresa's parents openly made love in front of Teresa, believing that if she was exposed to sex at a young age, she'd grow up thinking that it was a normal, beautiful act. Not surprisingly, though, her parents' behavior during intercourse frightened her.

That fear remains with Teresa today, and every time she makes love, the image of her parents' heaving, naked bodies enters her mind and disgusts her. Needless to say, this reaction interferes with Teresa's relationships with men, and at age 46 she worries that she'll never get married.

Her closest relationship is with food.

— Marcia's parents divorced when she was three, and she was raised by her beautiful young mother, who brought a succession of boyfriends home while Marcia was growing up. During her formative years, Marcia received a lot of advice from her mother with respect to men and dating—advice offered much too prematurely, given Marcia's age. Her mother was determined to groom Marcia to marry well, so she dressed the little girl in extremely seductive and sexually provocative outfits. She encouraged Marcia to wiggle her hips and wear make-up. "It's never too early to start," was her mother's motto. But, in truth, it *was* too early.

Marcia grew up thinking of herself as an object, destined

for men's pleasure and use. She didn't learn how to listen to her own inner desires and voice, and really had no idea what she wanted. Marcia only knew what men wanted and what her mother wanted. She was entirely outer-directed and gave the appearance of being a superficial, insincere people-pleaser.

Deep inside, Marcia's soul was screaming out for attention. In therapy, Marcia learned how to attend to her own needs and how to balance taking care of others with taking care of one's self. She had drowned out her soul's piteous cries with alcohol and food (she never binged, but she did pick on food all day long). However, as soon as she started paying attention to her own needs, Marcia's cravings for food and alcohol diminished.

— Like Marcia, Suzanne was raised by a single mother who regularly brought dates home. Growing up, Suzanne heard a lot of sexual sounds emanating from the bedroom, without having the maturity to understand what was going on. "I can still hear my mom screaming, 'Oh God, Oh God!'" Suzanne recalls. "To this day, I am totally silent when I make love with my husband, and I know it's because I don't want to be loud like my mom." Suzanne learned to fill up the silence within her with large amounts of food.

— Karen was also privy to inappropriate sexual material growing up, but instead of the muffled panting and moaning accompanying intercourse, she was subjected to dirty jokes and stories told by her father and her uncle during their weekend-afternoon drinking marathons. The men would insist that Karen listen as they reeled off their lewd tales, which she didn't find funny at all. "I guess they thought it was cute to watch a little girl's face contort and turn red with embarrassment," Karen painfully recounted.

"Sometimes, they would even ask me to memorize and repeat these jokes when friends would drop by. Everyone would get such a laugh out of it, but I was always so mad at my Dad for forcing me to hear and say these horrible, awful things. It was gross!"

Karen's anger and feelings of helplessness were compounded by the fact that her mother didn't "rescue her" from the clutches of her father's sick humor. And, the content of these jokes and stories also contributed to the low opinion that Karen formed about herself as she grew up. "Thanks to my Dad, I assumed that men thought of females exclusively as sex objects," she said. "So, I never pursued any relationships because I didn't want to just be some guy's 'hole,' which was how my Dad would refer to women."

Karen's weight topped 200 pounds before she reached age 21. Her Dad would joke about her weight and her extra-large breasts and buttocks. "I hid the hurt as best as I could," Karen recalled with tearing eyes. "But as soon as I had the opportunity, I'd eat to feel better."

— Deborah's mother, Anne, was a self-admitted flirt. At 43, Anne still thought of herself as attractive, but she actively sought male attention to bolster her aging ego. When Deborah started dating at age 15, Anne would flirt with her daughter's boyfriends. "At first I thought I was imagining it," remembers Deborah, "but after a while I saw how my Mom would dress really sexy whenever my boyfriend was supposed to come over. He even remarked to me once, 'Boy, you sure have a sexy Mom.' I was so embarrassed! Here, everybody else's mothers were normal housewives or working women. But my Mom thought she was Farrah Fawcett or something!"

By competing with her daughter for male sexual attention, Anne was committing a compound psychological crime. She was having a "mental affair" with Deborah's boyfriend, and she was also teaching her daughter unhealthy ways to relate to other women. Even today, Deborah has difficulty making friends with, and trusting, members of her own sex.

Deborah also internalized her mother's behavior in a way that negatively affected her own self-image. She negatively compared herself to Anne and other attractive women, believing she was "less than" they were. Deborah also mistrusted herself, a product of the way she felt about her mother while growing up.

Deborah, too, tried to suppress her pain through food. She was so sure that she was undesirable and unattractive that she didn't even try to maintain her looks or health through proper nutrition or exercise. "Why try?" was her motto.

— Kristy was also psychologically sexually abused. At age 12, Kristy began developing large breasts like her mother, and soon after, she started her period. That's when Kristy's mother had "a talk" with her.

"My mom told me how dirty and awful sex was," Kristy explained. "She said guys are only interested in one thing, and I must never ever give in until marriage. I mean, she went on and on about how sex was this horrible duty to perform for your husband."

When Kristy asked her mother for a training bra and permission to shave the coarse, dark hair on her legs, her mother reacted violently. "She slapped me!" said Kristy. "She said only sluts shaved their legs and wore bras. When I protested that she wore a bra and shaved her legs, she slapped me again. I never asked her another thing about sex."

Not surprisingly, Kristy became a teenage mother at age 16. Ignorant about birth control and eager to rebel against her mother, Kristy had slept with her boyfriend without using precautions. When she came to me for therapy, she was the unwed mother of three young children, and she felt angry and bitter about her life. Living in a trailer park, where she felt trapped and unhappy, she resorted to the only outlet for pleasure she could find—food. Today, at age 30, Kristy's weight tops 250 pounds.

— Jennifer's situation is, unfortunately, extremely common. Her father paid so much attention to Jennifer's maturing body that he, essentially, psychologically molested her.

For example, her father would constantly comment on her obviously budding breasts. "It felt creepy," Jennifer remembers, "knowing that my father was constantly checking me out. I mean, he'd talk about my boobs nonstop. It's practically like incest or something!"

While a father's attention during the sensitive adolescent transition period can, in some cases, be healthy and helpful, Jennifer's father's attentiveness triggered extreme self-consciousness in her. To conceal her breasts, she wore baggy sweaters and jackets, and if a boyfriend paid too much attention to her figure, Jennifer would scream at him.

Jennifer's subsequent obsession with dieting was a direct offshoot of her father's sexually laced attention. Both anorexics and compulsive dieters exhibit a fear of sexual attention, and often starve themselves into asexual little-boylike body shapes. In fact, they often lose so much body fat that their breasts, hips, and menstrual cycles practically disappear.

The Abuser's Role

The adults described in the aforementioned case studies on psychological sexual abuse acted irresponsibly toward their children. They hurt their offspring by marring their children's perspectives on relationships and healthy sexuality. As a result, they damaged their children's self-confidence.

It's doubtful that these adults intentionally tried to hurt their children. Most abusive parents whom I've worked with would not be considered categorically "bad people." Instead, they are oblivious, unaware, and clumsy—often the result of problems with alcohol, prescription or illegal drugs, or mental illness.

Later in this book, I'll delve more deeply into the hidden anger attached to abuse, but for now, I just want to make this crucial point: *Blaming* your parent or parents for having abused you won't serve any useful purpose. The worst thing you can do for yourself is to harbor resentment—that's a destructive emotion that will most assuredly trigger overeating episodes.

During the early stages of healing your pound/pain link, the most important thing is to *understand*—purely intellectually at this point— the source of the pain that led to your accumulation of excess weight. The feelings attached to that understanding definitely need to be dealt with. But not quite yet.

1st

Keep reading; you need to take each step in your recovery as it comes.

understand don't blame

Invisible Abuse?

In this chapter, we've focused on subtle forms of abuse up to this point. Psychological sexual abuse damages children, yet it's difficult to identify. Unlike a concrete physical act such as rape, molestation, or sodomy, the abuse described so far is almost invisible. Like a ghost, it haunts, frightens and scars its victims. And also like an apparition, these forms of abuse are difficult to describe and confront.

The adult abuser denies to him- or herself that a harmful act was committed. The abuser, most likely already suffering from low self-esteem, has a burning desire to be right all the time. If the abuser admits to a misdeed, the self-esteem is wounded even further.

In addition, the abuser's awareness of his or her abusive actions is often impaired by alcohol and drugs. One man I worked with had molested his daughter during an alcoholic blackout; he had no recollection of the event whatsoever. The man wasn't trying to escape responsibility for his actions—he was severely distressed by the incident. His alcoholism had simply blocked his conscious recollection of that deplorable act.

But getting back to more intangible forms of abuse, you can probably see how its very nature might make it difficult to pinpoint clearly and definitively. Not only are the more subtle forms of psychological abuse often repressed on the part of the abuser, but, as shown through the stories in this chapter, on the part of the victim, too. Whatever the degree of remorse on the part of the perpetrator, though, the victim still needs to deal with the pain and come to peace with herself.

Please don't get me wrong. I'm definitely not defending or justifying the abuser. In fact, I rarely work professionally with abusers because their level of sickness is so great, but those whom I have agreed to counsel were actively involved in recovery from alcoholism, drug addiction, and mental illnesses.

In any case, I do think that survivors of abuse can significantly contribute to their own healing by looking objectively at their abuser's motivations and mindset. As you read on, you might find that this level of objectivity will help *you* explore your own inner emotions and help you gain control over any feelings of rage you may be experiencing. By perceiving the abuser as a very sick person with a low level of awareness, you'll be better able to reframe your abuse history in a way that will bring you peace of mind. And with it, you can achieve freedom from overeating and weight gain.

You don't need to forgive the abuser. In fact, that would be unrealistic right now. But you do need to understand what happened to you in order to be free of pain. To be finally free.

Inappropriate Touching

A more tangible form of abuse often associated with overeating later in life takes the form of "inappropriate touching." Though not as blatant as crimes such as rape or incest, Amy's case will illustrate how this type of sexual abuse "ghost" can still shatter a child's trust and self-image.

— Amy was a strikingly beautiful brunette with a master's degree in chemistry. In her prestigious research position at the local university, Amy had achieved much success and had been published in several professional journals. Yet, for all her accomplishments, Amy did not feel good about herself when she came in to see me for psychotherapy.

As we delved into Amy's history, some powerfully negative feelings surfaced. First, Amy acknowledged her ambivalent feelings toward her body. She always wore very masculine, boxy suits to work, ostensibly for the sake of maintaining professionalism. But in truth, Amy's fear of attracting male sexual attention made her choose the unattractive, oversized suits she wore. Even on personal trips out of town, where no colleague could possibly see her, she wore unflattering clothing.

But her fashion choices were only the most visible symptoms of Amy's confusion with respect to her self-image. Below the surface, Amy was dealing with many more issues. First, she was intensely jealous of any woman she considered attractive, especially provocatively dressed women. Amy was so threatened by females whom she perceived in this way that she'd actually broken up with three boyfriends whom she had unjustly accused of infidelity. In all three cases, Amy's insecurity had precipitated bitter, jealous fights.

"I always felt that my boyfriends would rather be with a prettier woman," Amy recalled. She described a typical example of her jealousy-based relationship problems: Amy and her most recent boyfriend, Ronald, a teacher at the university, were walking around the university campus on a beautiful autumn afternoon. Everything had been perfect—the weather, the scenery, the conversation. Everything, that is, until Amy spotted a curvy coed approaching the couple.

It was one of Ronald's students, who asked him a question about a homework assignment. Their conversation was brief, but Amy was red-faced with rage by the time the student walked away. She blew up at Ronald, accusing him of flirting with the girl, of having inappropriate relationships with his students. Ronald tried to defend himself, but Amy stormed off.

"And that's pretty much how most of my relationships end," she said quietly. "I just get so jealous that I blow up."

We focused on Amy's conflicting feelings about allowing herself to be attractive. She discussed her fears, which were triggered when men flirted with her. She discussed her fears of being attractive, and her fears of not being attractive.

In my work with abuse survivors, I constantly see this femininity ambivalence. An offshoot of society's madonna-whore paradox where women feel pressured to "be virginal, but be sexy and attractive," Amy's confusion centered on how she fit into this loop. As a professional woman in a "man's field," Amy fought to be taken seriously, so she wore a man's uniform to disguise the femininity that she linked with weakness.

Now, while it's true that wearing short skirts and tight sweaters can spell professional suicide in circles such as Amy's, she could have worn fashionable, well-fitting suits without sacrificing the respect of her peers.

You see, clothing is very much a symbol and an indicator of self-esteem. Women such as Amy who "hide" themselves in baggy clothing often harbor deep fears of femininity and male sexual attention. Conversely, women who usually wear tight, provocative clothing may fear rejection and have a marked need for attention. And, interestingly enough, women who make a habit of wearing raggedy old bras and panties are exhibiting a form of self-contempt, but that's another subject.

In Amy's case, her fears about female sexuality stemmed from an incident that occurred while she was in her teens. Although Amy downplayed its significance at first, saying, "Oh, it just happened once," or "I think I was imagining it happened," or "I'm really making too big a deal out of nothing," the fact that she thought about it regularly signified its importance.

What happened was this: When Amy was 14, her favorite uncle, who was 29, very cute, and whom she had a crush on, was at the house for a family dinner. Amy had looked forward to seeing him all day, and she took extra care to brush her hair into a pretty braid and to wear the new dress she'd received at Christmas. Deep green velvet, the dress perfectly skimmed over her slim hips and budding breasts, making her look like a young beauty queen.

When Amy made her entrance into the kitchen, where her uncle was seated, the impact was enormous. He let out an appreciative whistle and said, "Amy, if you weren't my cousin, I'd ask you out on a date right now." Amy's heart skipped a beat and she blushed. She felt shy, at a loss for words.

Her uncle wasn't shy, though. In fact, the more beer he drank, the louder and bolder his flirtations became. Then it happened. After dinner, Amy was washing dishes at the sink, and her uncle came over and stood next to her, breathing his hot beer breath on her neck. She could sense impending trouble, but she didn't move away.

He proceeded to put his arm around her and kiss her on the cheek. As he kissed her, his hand dropped down to her breast and he squeezed it, full-on, with his whole hand.

Amy dropped her dish towel and ran silently to her bedroom. She ripped off her green velvet dress and kicked it into a little ball, pushing it to the back of her closet. When she rediscovered the dress a month later, she threw it in the trash.

Amy never wore pretty dresses after that. She gradually stopped wearing anything that risked attracting male attention. In therapy, I helped Amy acknowledge the importance of what had happened to her back then. While to some teenagers, this incident might have been inconsequential, for a girl as sensitive as Amy the situation served to paralyze her with fear and shame about being an attractive woman. As a result, she refused to allow herself to express her feminine side and tended to resent those women who could.

For Amy, the incident was anything but small.

Now, why am I including this case study in this book? After all, Amy did not have an eating disorder as much as she had a distorted image of herself, both physically and emotionally. Well, the reason is that this type of distortion is usually associated with women who overeat. Instead of wearing ill-fitting clothing, many women hide their femininity in mounds of extra pounds.

Inappropriate touching is a not-so-subtle form of abuse that leaves its victims feeling dirty and ashamed. They blame themselves for attracting the unwanted advance, and then proceed to downplay the situation, saying, "Maybe I just imagined that he touched me there. Maybe it was just an accident."

Whatever the rationalization, the end result is the same: A victim of inappropriate touching takes responsibility for an act that she did not bring upon herself, and instead of directing her anger toward the abuser, she turns the anger toward herself.

You'll learn how to release this type of anger in the second part of this book.

C   H   A   P   T   E   R   S   E   V   E   N

VIOLATED AT HOME

"True courage is like a kite; a contrary wind raises it higher."
> —John Petit-Senn, philosopher/author

INCEST.

The word alone makes one shudder. It is a monstrous act—that of an adult violating the trust of a child, especially a child who is related to the adult by blood. Yet, incest in its many forms is more common than we can imagine. And fathers, stepfathers, uncles, brothers, and even mothers, aunts, and sisters are usually the perpetrators of this pernicious form of sexual abuse.

Research, and my own clinical experience, both point to enormous emotional and psychological transformations in children who are subject to acts of incest. Guilt and self-blame are usually integral elements of the incest survivor's pain. As evinced below, my client Joanne's reaction to an incestuous experience is tragically common among those who experience this type of abuse.

— When Joanne came to me for treatment, she was what we in this profession refer to as "therapy-wise." She had seen four or five other therapists before me, and had checked in and out of psychiatric hospitals. Joanne had told her story so many times that she recounted it without showing a trace of emotion.

She told me how her then-20-year-old uncle—her

father's brother—would spend every summer with the family. When she was six years old, he began "seducing" Joanne. First, he would hold her on his lap. Then, he would take her in her bedroom and give her long, pleasurable back rubs. Joanne, the oldest of four siblings, loved all the attention that her uncle showered on her. She even developed a little crush on him.

One day, Joanne's uncle was rubbing her back. He asked her to take her clothes off so he could give me "an extra-special massage." Joanne gladly obliged, and that's when her uncle's fingers began exploring her genitals. Joanne haltingly describes the next part: it's obvious she's confused and conflicted about her feelings.

On the one hand, the attention was emotionally delicious to Joanne. No adult had ever been so attentive to her before. And, on a purely physical level, the back rubs were wonderful. She had opened her heart and emotions to her uncle—Joanne trusted him completely.

Then he violated that trust by touching her genitals. But Joanne ignored her natural feelings of alarm and panic, and only paid attention to the pleasurable physical sensations that his fingers evoked. She felt erotically aroused, even though her stomach ached at the thought that "this isn't right." At the same time, her uncle reassured Joanne that he loved her and that she was his special princess.

Every summer, the incestuous acts would escalate. By the time she was 11 years old, Joanne and her uncle were engaging in sexual intercourse on a regular basis, and she was becoming increasingly confused. On the one hand, Joanne craved her uncle's attention and love, and she even enjoyed the physical sensations of sex, for the most part. But the secrecy surrounding their relationship, pounded home by her uncle's warning, "Don't you ever tell no one about us, you hear?," reminded Joanne that what they were doing was very, very wrong.

Joanne began eating in secret, as she felt more and more isolated from her family. With no one to confide in, food functioned as her solace, her companion. She gained so much weight that her uncle actually rejected her as being "too fat" when he arrived for the summer prior to her 13th birthday. This rejection escalated the extent of Joanne's secret eating even more.

Clearly, Joanne's incestuous relationship had deeply penetrated her self-image; yet, she told me her story as casually as if she were describing a shopping expedition. Again, this is a normal reaction in incest survivors, who have assimilated the "thorn in their paw" as if it were a normal part of life. They are, sadly, used to living with pain.

Guilt and Self-Blame

Deep down, Joanne believed that she contributed to the incest. "I could have stopped it if I had wanted to," was her recurring thought. "But I didn't stop it because part of me enjoyed it, so it must be my fault. I can't blame my uncle for what happened."

I've heard so many incest survivors echo Joanne's sentiments. They say, "It's my fault because . . .

. . . I didn't say no."

. . . I acted seductively."

. . . I enjoyed it."

. . . I didn't tell anyone."

. . . we had a special relationship."

As adults, we must take responsibility for our own actions. But, when we are children, are we responsible for our *inter*actions with adults? Isn't the adult the person truly responsible for the outcome of situations involving children? The adult, after all, is the one who controls the tempo, tone, and flavor of any situation. The adult has the power to coerce, force, and generally manipulate the child into doing whatever is intended. The adult can also create the illusion that the child is a willing partner.

For so many incest, molestation, and rape survivors, the basic human response to sexual arousal creates guilt and self-blame. From a physiological standpoint, if someone touches our genitals in a certain way, we become aroused. Our breathing becomes shallow and fast, our heart and pulse rates quicken, our vaginal walls thicken, and we excrete lubrication. We also feel pleasurable sensations in the clitoral region.

These feelings represent a physiological fact of life, yet sexual trauma survivors bear tremendous guilt as a result of these very human reactions. "I felt turned on," is the irrational logic, "so I must have contributed to the situation." The reality, of course, is that these victims were anything but consensual partners.

It may help to envision a pipeline running through your body, from the top of your head and out through your toes. This pipeline is what our normal human emotions run through. Normally, an emotion occurs, we feel energized by the feeling, and then the feeling dissipates and runs out the bottom of the pipeline.

Now, imagine that pipeline being clogged. Emotions become backed up, like stopped-up plumbing in a sink. Well, that's exactly what happens when guilt and self-blame occur—they act like blocks in our emotional pipeline, backing up strong feelings behind them.

The incest survivor blames herself. She also isolates herself—rarely, if ever, revealing what transpired. If she does talk about it, she distances herself from the emotions connected to the incest, just as she did when the trauma originally occurred. During an incestuous encounter, children "shut off" their painful feelings of alarm and shame. Later, when they remember the incidents, these feelings usually remain detached from their true inner self.

The incest survivor usually feels "different" from other girls her age. She often feels damaged, as if something is terribly wrong with her. And she suspects that other people, even strangers, know that something's amiss. She expects to be rejected, disliked, and mistreated by others. She doesn't know the meaning of a trusting, intimate relationship where she can let her guard down.

So much isolation, so much self-loathing. The only way the incest survivor can concentrate on her adult responsibilities is to close down all memories and emotions connected to the original pain. This is one of the primary reasons why she overeats. Food makes her feel numb and keeps the memories and emotions from surfacing. It also serves as a form of entertainment to counteract the boredom caused by her isolation, and gives her companionship and a feeling of "fullness" in contrast to the emptiness coursing through her soul.

If *you* are a person experiencing acute, stinging emotional pain, you are probably aware that food is a very quick fix. You're in so much pain that you quit caring whether you'll gain weight or not. You give up. You just want to feel better NOW, and you know exactly what will do it. Food. Then, when the satisfying effects of overeating wear off, you eat some more.

Food Helps You Forget

Food not only makes you feel calm and numb, it also quiets troublesome thoughts and memories. Take Cheryl's case, for example:

> — Cheryl was depressed and having trouble losing weight when she checked into the women's psychiatric hospital where I was Program Director. I worked closely with her to uncover her true issues.
>
> A bright, highly educated woman, Cheryl's extra 50 pounds came from one primary source: the case of colas she consumed every day. She almost always had a can of cola in her hand, and she sipped on it continually. What purpose was the cola serving? I wondered.
>
> Since Cheryl had been through years of outpatient therapy, she was another "therapy-wise" client. She'd read dozens of self-help books and taken numerous psychology classes in college. She was also terrified by the prospect of unearthing the pain she could feel just below the surface,

deep inside of her. Cheryl's defenses were high, guarding against any undue anguish.

When Cheryl told me that she couldn't remember her childhood before age 12, I knew immediately that she was repressing some dreadful memories with her selective amnesia. Forgetting, you see, is not something that people do of their own volition; rather, it is a coping mechanism that allows them to avoid facing painful truths about their lives.

We decided that hypnosis would be an effective way of accessing Cheryl's hidden memories. During the first session, I asked Cheryl to describe the house she'd grown up in. She described it in brilliant detail, vividly giving me a "mental tour" of her house. Then, when I asked her to take me into her bedroom, she stopped. Another clue. She couldn't remember her bedroom.

The second session did yield a few details about Cheryl's bedroom, though. She described waking up on a summer morning, with the light streaming in through her window. Now we had an "anchor," or a starting place, to initiate her memory retrieval, but she was still blocked.

I suspected that the colas were helping Cheryl silence her memories and feelings, so she agreed to abstain from all soda pop or other carbonated beverages. Since she was staying at the hospital, it was easier for her to adhere to this resolution.

Body Memories of Abuse

By the time of our next session, Cheryl had been abstaining from colas for two days, and suddenly the memories started flowing. Now, as I mentioned in a previous chapter, there is a lot of controversy these days with respect to therapists possibly "planting" ideas in clients' minds, especially where repressed memories of sexual abuse are concerned. I have seen overzealous, inexperienced counselors encourage clients to "recall" events that probably never happened. In fact, I've seen at least two clients diagnosed as having a "multiple personality disorder" when it was unwarranted.

In Cheryl's case, her story was definitely her own; it was flowing from her without any prompting on my part. I played the part of a "blank slate therapist," one who neither exhibits pleasure or displeasure while listening to what my client has to say. By doing so, the client is less apt to try to please the therapist by saying what she thinks the therapist wants to hear. Since compulsive overeaters are extremely sensitive to the reactions of other people (more than they are to their own), it's important for therapists to remain neutral with clients— warm, but neutral.

As Cheryl continued telling her story, she remembered her father coming into her bedroom while her mother was at work. He had been drinking and looked strange, with a faraway expression in his bloodshot eyes. Cheryl's father didn't waste any time: he pulled out his erect penis and forced Cheryl to take it in her mouth. He ejaculated almost immediately, and then left the bedroom, with Cheryl throwing up the semen onto her pillow.

She was terrified. Too frightened to confront her father after the fact or tell her mother what had happened. An only child without any other relatives, Cheryl didn't know whom to turn to. So she chose to forget. It never happened again, and her father never mentioned it. He died when Cheryl was 45, with the two never having mentioned what had transpired between them. For all Cheryl knew, her father may have been so drunk at the time that he may not have even remembered it himself.

I concluded that Cheryl's compulsion to drink soda was a reaction to the ejaculate in her mouth. As soon as we took the soda away, she began remembering. Her first clear memory was the sensation of her father's sharp pubic hairs pressed against her face. She kept saying, "It hurts, it hurts," during her early hypnosis sessions, so we made an effort to uncover the source of this "hurt." As soon as she remembered that it was her father's sharp pubic hair pressed hard against her face that caused the pain, she started to cry.

Cheryl allowed herself to recall the rest of the memories of that incident over the next two sessions. We learned that the colas had served to suppress the "body memories" of the incident—the sharp pubic hairs, the smell of sweat and semen, and the taste and sensation of ejaculate. The carbonation overrode the memories that she was cognizant of on a deeper level.

It's very common for the body to have haunting sensations, or "body memories," long after a trauma has occurred. Incest survivors who endure vaginal penetration often have gynecological disorders. I've worked with two survivors of forced anal sex who had colon problems. The body is crying out; it wants you to remember and release the pain.

When Cheryl finally did remember, and then released her pain in the ways described later on in this book, she didn't *need* colas anymore. Her subconscious need to "cleanse" her mouth with cola was obviated. And, since her caloric intake dropped dramatically, so too did her weight.

"I Don't Remember!"

What if—as in Cheryl's case—you *suspect* that you've been sexually abused, but you can't remember any specific incident? Well, there is no one right answer to that question. All I can do is present you with available options, and then you must choose which path is right for *you*.

There are many different schools of thought about repressed sexual abuse memories, especially in the past year, as "false memory syndrome" has made the news. Ellen Bass, a respected writer in the San Francisco Bay area and co-author of the classic work on sexual abuse, *The Courage to Heal,* told me this: "If a woman thinks she's been sexually abused, then she has. Period." Bass believes that no one thinks about sexual abuse in the absence of actual abuse occurring.

Other therapists scoff at this idea and actually go to the other extreme. One male psychiatrist told me that, in his view, memories of sexual abuse are often women's "fantasies of having sex with their fathers. It's a projection of their true wishes." Now, this theory—widely held by many Freudian psychiatrists—is dangerous, as far as I'm concerned! I understand, and to some degree, accept, the Oedipus and Electra complex theories (that we, as children, perceive our parents as ideal love objects). But I don't think that our love for our fathers would lead to fantasized images of forced, painful sex! This implication simply revictimizes the victim and causes her additional anguish. Sexual abuse survivors feel guilty enough, without having a psychiatrist tell them that they made the whole thing up because they really wanted to have sex with their fathers!

To me, the truth lies somewhere in between the psychiatric model and Bass's theory. During my work with abuse survivors, I have been struck by the fact that everyone remembered their abuse *when they were ready*. I've worked with survivors in the 40- to 60-year-old age range who have lived their whole lives—holding jobs and raising families—without remembering their abuse.

Then, at some point in their lives, an amazing thing happened. The survivor had a glimmer of a memory, a fleeting picture of her father holding them down, or her brother's naked body. Some minuscule image, connected to powerful feelings of fear or rage, prompted the rest of the memories to pour out. She is haunted by disturbing memories and feelings of overwhelming grief for days, sometimes weeks, until she remembers everything.

It is clear that she was ready to remember.

I do believe that the quality of life improves dramatically once the memory is retrieved and the emotions have been worked through. Many middle-aged and elderly clients I've worked with have expressed remorse that they didn't get into therapy at an earlier age. They probably would have been lighter, happier, and freer throughout the course of their lives had they tackled their sexual abuse issues years before. Their overeating and weight gain would have presented less of a problem; in fact, they might not have been factors in their lives to begin with.

However, just as you can't unfurl the petals of a rose and make it bloom before it's ready, I don't think it's wise to force a survivor to remember before she's at the right place in her personal growth. She'll enter therapy when she's feeling pain too great to handle on her own.

Pain is a gift that forces us to do good things for ourselves—I truly believe that. Throughout her life, a woman who has endured an abusive situation often tends to focus on the needs of others. The only thing that makes her pay attention to herself is if her body SCREAMS at her through the conduit of emotional or physical pain. Her body and emotions demand that she listen.

In other words, the body is a perfectly engineered clock. Although selective amnesia is an incredible coping device, graciously allowing victims some semblance of sanity and peace of mind, the clock knows when it's time to remember. And it's a good thing it does, because a repressed memory is like a dormant volcano, with the lava of anger toward one's self and the perpetrator bubbling below the surface.

This below-the-surface activity creates a paradox. An island with a dormant volcano may appear to be paradise, but that is an illusion because there is actually a continual building-up of tension as the inevitable explosion looms ahead. An abuse survivor with repressed memories is living with the same uneasiness—she may appear to have a happy, full life, but there is always something going on below the surface, something pervasive and menacing that leaves her soul hungry for freedom, happiness—and food.

Some Clues to Help You

If you suspect that you were sexually abused but are not quite sure, some detective work might be in order. Detectives, of course, use deductive reasoning to solve cases. Deductive reasoning means starting with a lot of clues and information and then narrowing the focus to only the most important facts. You can do the same thing.

To help you in your detective work, I have listed some traits, characteristics, and outcomes commonly exhibited by sexual abuse survivors. A word of caution, though: Many of these traits characterize other types of childhood trauma other than sexual abuse. So, use this list for general information only. If you already strongly suspect you were sexually abused and, in addition, you relate to the majority of traits in the list, *then* I would recommend exploring the issue further with a therapist trained in abuse counseling.

❧ Traits and Characteristics Often Exhibited by ❧ Sexual Abuse Survivors

Eating Disorders: Compulsive overeating, chronic dieting, yo-yo syndrome, anorexia, bulimia

Chemical Dependency: Alcohol abuse, drug addiction, prescription drug abuse

Sexual Dysfunction: Promiscuity, avoidance of all sex, pain during intercourse, inability or extreme difficulty achieving orgasm

Sleep Disorders: Chronic nightmares, insomnia, oversleeping, lethargy

Lifestyle Issues: Inability to hold job, chronic financial and legal problems, prostitution, irresponsibility, being disorganized or organized to a fault

Relationship Signals: Extreme rage toward one or more parents, inability to trust others, irrational fear of abandonment, insatiable need for reassurance and proof of love, jealousy, suspicion, contempt for men

Body Image Concerns: Compulsion to exercise and weigh oneself, avoidance of all exercise, obsession with plastic surgery, perfectionism with respect to dress and appearance

Social Issues: People-pleasing or complete isolation from others, being very guarded and self-protective, feeling a need to be in control of all situations, being compulsively late or punctual, self-centeredness or self-consciousness, grandiosity mixed with very low self-esteem, difficulty laughing or expressing any emotion, laughing too much as an obvious avoidance tactic

Health Signals: Chronic gynecological problems, colonic or rectal disorders

Most of these characteristics or traits involve normal behavior that is taken to the extreme, so, again, it's important not to read too much into this list. It's not necessary for you to categorically label yourself as "a sexual abuse survivor" or not. What *is* of the utmost importance is uncovering and releasing whatever pain is triggering your overeating tendencies.

Coming to Grips with the Unthinkable

Another client, Delores, had abstained from her binge foods (high-fat cheeseburgers and french fries) for two weeks before her memories of incest came flooding to the surface. She was in a group therapy session at our outpatient clinic when she began crying, then screaming hysterically, all the while keeping her eyes tightly shut.

When she'd calmed down a bit, she told the group about the horrible image she'd just seen flashing through her mind: She remembered her father sodomizing her when she was a little girl. Although Delores knew that her sister had been her father's victim of incest and had been in therapy for years, Delores thought that she'd come out untouched. What had actually happened, though, was that she'd blocked the memories of those few horrible times that her father had forced her to have anal sex.

She'd focused all her energies, instead, on helping her younger sister with her problems. Delores had always concentrated on other people, which was another way—besides overeating—to stifle her own thoughts. She joined our program because her co-workers were losing weight at our clinic. "If I could only lose 50 pounds, then I'd be happy," was her initial statement to the intake therapist. We never argue with clients when we hear this statement, although we hear it all the time. We just let matters proceed along their course.

It's true that for some people, overweight may be purely tied to genetics, slow thyroids, or sluggish metabolisms. It just so happens I have yet to meet anyone with those problems. Once they release the food (or beverages) that serve as a protective shield, every client whom I've ever worked with has uncovered hidden memories or emotions that have eventually surfaced.

Of course, in some cases, the memories are already on the surface. My client, Terry, for instance, remembered every detail of the incest sessions she had with her father and uncle. The trouble was, she recalled the incidents intellectually, without feeling any of the accompanying emotions. This is a phenomenon that I see all the time, a very common scenario.

An incest survivor will often insist that "it was no big deal." She has a powerful need to see herself as a strong survivor—which she certainly is. Because, in order to survive incest—an utter betrayal of trust on the part of a family member—one has to deal with one of the most excruciating traumas imaginable. But incest doesn't just make you stop trusting others; it makes you mistrust yourself. You become guarded, defensive, isolated, tough.

Talk-show hostess Oprah Winfrey has publicly discussed her own history of incest. Her uncle molested her in rural Tennessee, and although Oprah remembered and acknowledged the incest, it was in that emotionally devoid, intellectually based manner that I see time and time again. And that's precisely why, after she lost all that weight on Opti-Fast, she gained it all back again.

She hadn't yet released her pain. But more on that topic later in this chapter. I want to get back to Terry.

— Terry grew up in the county next to where Oprah Winfrey was raised. She lived with her parents and an extended family out in the middle of nowhere, in a large farmhouse. There was no school in the vicinity, so Terry was schooled at home. Home is also where she was subjected to a horrible custom that was all too common in rural parts of the country.

She recounted what had happened to her when she was a little girl: "My uncle took me into his bedroom and said, 'Now it's time for you to become a lady.' Then he took off my clothes and underwear and he . . . he had sex with me. It hurt really, really bad. I was crying, but he wouldn't stop.

"Two days later, my father did the same thing. I had sex regularly with my uncle and my father. My mother and everyone else knew all about it, but everyone just accepted it. That's just the way things were done. My mother had sex with her father, and her mother had done the same before her. It's so sick, now that I know better, but it was a family custom."

Whenever Terry's father and uncle wanted sex, they'd tell Terry that it was "special time," and she'd dutifully comply with their wishes. Years later, when Terry was enrolled in a public junior high school, she asked a classmate if she ever had "special times" with her father. "Sure," the girl replied. "Whenever my father and I go fishing together, that's a very special time."

Terry realized that her friend's "special time" with her dad was quite different from the "special time" that she was having with her own father. After probing further, and without revealing why she was asking, Terry discovered that her incestuous relationship was not normal at all.

Terry's only way out was to run away, and she became a street urchin of sorts, trying to survive by hustling and begging. She even sold her body for sex on a couple of occasions, just to get enough money to eat. By the time Terry checked into our psychiatric hospital, she had tried to commit suicide several times.

Terry was the ultimate "tough chick." Her short-cropped black hair and ultra-masculine clothing, combined with her ever-present scowl, gave her a menacing presence. No one, but no one was going to get close to Terry. She pushed everyone away who tried to help her, screaming at the nurses and cussing at the counselors.

This behavior was a clue to what was actually going on inside, because often those who are the most unlovable are the ones who need the most love. Terry was definitely vying for the title, "Most Unlovable," and I knew that that meant she needed extra love from others. The hospital staff ignored her rude comments and, instead, showered her with kind words and affection. We also asked her to put her thoughts down in a journal (we couldn't ask her to express *feelings* yet, as she wasn't in touch with them, and this request would have frustrated her).

Every night, Terry would pour her heart out into her journal. The next day, she would ask me to read her journal entries. I knew what she wanted: she was asking me to understand her. As much as Terry feared getting close to people, she also craved emotional intimacy. All people do. After all, connecting with others is a normal human need—that's why solitary confinement is the ultimate punishment in prison.

What follows is one of Terry's journal entries, which told me, as well as the other staff members, that Terry was getting in touch with her true self. Keep in mind that Terry was 37 years old at the time she wrote this:

I am a child. I know this because it is said that emotionally one stops growing up when child abuse starts. Well, that made sense to me. That gave me the answer to why I had a hard time coming across right with emotionally mature adults, and why I couldn't understand where the heck they were coming from.

My abuse started at the age of three or younger. I was drinking whiskey from a bottle by what I had been told, when I was a little baby. So, how do I grow up? I wanted to just hurry and grow up! So . . . I worked hard in therapy, I read and studied recovery books, went to all the suggested meetings, and I put a lot of time every day into all these things so I could grow up real fast.

I couldn't understand it! I still threw fits of anger when I felt rejected or hurt. I still felt empty inside, and I have been getting hugs from people, and people like me. I still hated myself when I knew that I really was okay. I couldn't get my head to catch up to my emotions.

But . . . I have grown up some now. I can see that I am defensive, and I can see that I am not coming across on the outside the way I really feel on the inside. Like for example, when I don't like myself, I come across like the kid that says: No. I don't want anything. Go away. I don't always catch my attitude at the time, because I am into my own thoughts and feelings and not paying attention to how my actions are being perceived. And that makes me feel worse, and so I hurt myself, isolate, be harder on me still.

I know that part of growing up is learning how to take responsibility for my own actions. Heck, I would hit myself, starve myself, binge on food until my stomach hurts, send people away from me, and even just go try and die, so I wouldn't feel so bad about messing up!

Terry was clearly craving human interaction. At the same time, she saw herself as being very different—even inferior to—other people. She wanted to be accepted, but was terrified of being rejected or abandoned, so the bottom line was that she couldn't stand any more hurt, so she had to avoid any situation that was potentially painful. And as painful as loneliness is, it hurts less than being rejected, so instead of risking rejection, Terry rejected others first.

As insensitive as Terry seemed to the outside world, she was exquisitely sensitive on the inside. In another journal entry, Terry chronicled her struggle with her vulnerability issues:

> *I do not want to admit that I am in need of support, that I can't handle things all on my own, the way I think I should be able to handle them. So . . . I don't tell anyone.*
>
> *I even have found myself griping about things that don't even matter, coming across in a hatred way even with nit-picky things, trying to detach from the love and the caring that I have for [the hospital staff]. Even when I get a hug from you, I then run away. And I am still having a hard time with letting you all know my needs, and so I just let you all think that I am not needing anything, even when you ask me, and I end up in crisis from not getting those needs met. Then I tell you when it's almost too late.*
>
> *When I am mad at myself, I definitely don't want any of you around me, because you don't deserve to be around someone so bad as me, and I may even have the face of anger, but it's not toward any of you. It is toward me.*

Trusting Others, Trusting Self

Terry, like so many other sexual abuse survivors, was struggling with trust issues. Human beings learn how to trust others from the moment they're born. Normally, a baby cries, and her mother or father takes care of her needs. She learns that the world responds to her and takes care of her.

A baby or child who is sexually violated feels physical pain—it *hurts* to have foreign objects inserted into your vaginal or anal regions. So, she cries. But the pain doesn't stop—instead, it gets worse.

If a parent is the sexual abuser, the child's ability to trust may be shattered to the point where trusting *anyone*—even her own self— seems impossible. After all, if you can't trust Mommy or Daddy, how can you learn to trust anybody at all?

If someone other than a parent is the sexual abuser, the child still feels that her trust was violated. I've worked with people who were sexually abused by adult authority figures such as doctors, teachers, priests, and baby-sitters, and they were shattered by the experience. Usually, trust is then replaced with fear. This person trusted an adult to treat her nicely, and that trust was betrayed. In addition, she in- stinctively wonders why Mommy and Daddy didn't protect her from the abuser.

There's Not Enough Chocolate in the World . . .

Most of the early childhood sexual abuse survivors I've worked with described feeling something akin to a "big empty hole" in the center of their being. They felt empty and incomplete, and there was an urge to relieve the feeling of emptiness, as well as the self-doubt, fear, and anger that resided there. The best way they could think of to fill that hole was by eating a lot of fattening, starchy foods. And, in some cases, other types of compulsive behavior, such as shopping, drink- ing, or addictive relationships took the place of compulsive overeating.

But nothing, nothing ever completely fills the chasm. There just isn't enough chocolate cake in the world to quiet the pangs of emptiness. No matter how much she eats, the abuse survivor can't escape the echoes emanating from the hollow drum in her middle.

I've always remembered the line from the play, *Les Miserables*: "There's a grief that can't be spoken. There's a pain, goes on and on." Well, for abuse survivors, the emotional pain that they feel is beyond words. It's a chronic, intense gnawing that they've almost gotten used

100 ?

to as a result of living with it for so long. But, a basic instinct of living creatures is to extinguish pain when one feels it. An animal whose foot is caught in a trap will chew off his limb to escape. Abuse survivors who compulsively overeat are doing the same thing.

You see, when your overeating stems from emotional need, there's an urgency attached to this behavior. And a seemingly endless emptiness and hunger. No matter how much you eat, you never feel full or satisfied. You want more food, more sedation, more comfort, more love.

Food temporarily relieves the hollow feeling within you, but not for long. It's as if you are being hypnotized by food, and as soon as the hypnotic trance is broken, you need more food to remain in a state of not-so-blissful ignorance.

But there *is* a way out of this maze. I promise you.

ADOLESCENT AND ADULTHOOD
SEXUAL TRAUMAS

"Nothing in life is to be feared. It is only to be understood."

—Madame Curie

WHILE A CHILD is particularly vulnerable to abuse due to her small stature and trusting, innocent nature, adolescents and adults are also ripe for psychological and physical abuse.

Dating and/or marrying the wrong man is one of the primary factors leading to an abusive situation in a woman's life—my own included. Many women will become involved with a man who, at first glance, seems to be the epitome of Prince Charming. Only later do we discover his dark, stormy side. A woman who was fortunate enough to be raised in a loving, supportive family devoid of abuse will recognize the man as someone who is sick and in need of professional help. Such a woman will then take one of two avenues: she will either insist that the sick man receive help of some kind, or she will leave him. Only a woman who grew up thinking that abuse is normal would try to change, or stay in a relationship with, a morose or volatile man.

Yet, many women do stay with abusive boyfriends and husbands through hell and high water—mostly through hell. And while I only advocate divorce as a last-ditch measure, many of my clients have found that that was the only way to end their pain. Of course, divorce and romantic break-ups bring on a new set of problems altogether, which is why many women continue to overeat even after leaving abusive men. Divorce doesn't automatically create rainbows in the sky and birds merrily chirping in the trees. However, I have certainly witnessed a lot of positive changes occurring in women who extricated themselves from bad marriages.

"You Would If You Loved Me": Abusive Boyfriends

Melody, a stunning 19-year-old blue-eyed blonde, was in my office crying uncontrollably. Her boyfriend Mark had just dropped her off for her psychotherapy session, and they'd had an intense argument on the way over.

"He called me a . . . a . . ."—she could barely say the words— ". . . a fucking bitch!" Melody cried, her face contorted with shock and rage. "Nobody has ever, ever called me that before!" She continued blowing her nose and rocking herself in my office chair.

Why do young women such as Melody, the image of beauty and promise, become attracted to, and then remain with, abusive boyfriends such as Mark? Unfortunately, the majority of teen clients I've worked with are just like Melody—crushed by low self-esteem, and counting on a "cool" boyfriend to provide love, companionship, and social status. What they usually don't bargain for is the hot temper and insensitive nature often common to these "cool guys."

Mark, like many of my clients' boyfriends, smoked marijuana and drank beer daily. Naturally, he downplayed the impact that these drugs had on his moods: "It's just pot and beer; at least it ain't crack cocaine and hard liquor!"

But marijuana, as I've found through working with people with addictive personalities, is often the cause of erratic mood swings. After lighting up a joint, the pot smoker can be calm and euphoric and pleasant to be around, or he can be silly, immature, and obnoxious. After he comes down, he is often extremely touchy, grouchy, and irritable. As a result, his girlfriend has to walk on eggshells around him to avoid triggering a verbal tirade or physical battery.

However, the pot smoker will swear that this isn't so. "Just give me another joint and I'll be normal again," he'll say. Then we therapists are left to pick up the pieces when their girlfriends are victimized by psychological or physical abuse once again.

So, I reiterate: Why would a girl or woman want to associate with a guy who treats her with a lack of respect? The answer, of course, is that she has either grown up believing that this sort of abuse is normal or, because she doesn't believe that she deserves—or can find—anyone better. In addition, she probably blames herself for the man's harsh words and actions.

"If only I: "lose weight," "look sexier," "act sweeter," "give him oral sex," and so on, then he'll treat me better." She desperately wants to be able to predict and control his outbursts of temper. Occasionally, when she finds something that seems to work ("I fixed him his favorite dinner, and he calmed down"), she'll become unrealistically attached to that behavior. Unfortunately, the man soon finds something else to be upset about, and she has to start all over again, looking for the magic formula to counter his unpredictable moods.

My work with young women such as Melody involves buoying up their self-esteem (almost to the extreme), and trying to provide the best advice for the situation. And while I couldn't tell Melody to leave Mark, I did urge her to protect herself against pregnancy. It is heartbreaking to see a woman in an insecure relationship get pregnant and then decide that she has no choice but to marry the baby's father. This situation points to the inevitability of divorce, and by that time, she may have borne additional children whom she will have to support.

What follows are some of the poignant stories of young women I've worked with who carried pounds of pain triggered by boyfriend abuse.

— Yolanda complained that Bob, her new boyfriend, "was never around." When I asked her to expand on this statement, she revealed that Bob was actually dating—and sleeping with—two other young women. "He says he loves all of us," Yolanda told me. "He says he can't decide who he should marry, so he needs to date all of us. He needs to . . . go to bed with all of us, and then he'll decide which one of us to pick."

The insecurities that Yolanda had developed while waiting to be "chosen" as the winner of this sick beauty contest had driven her to snack incessantly on fattening snacks such as chips, pretzels, and nuts. She'd actually gained ten pounds within a month, a fact that did not go unnoticed by Bob. "He complained that my butt's getting too big," Yolanda blurted out with a pained expression on her face. "I know if I get fat, Bob won't pick me, but I can't stay away from eating!"

— Lucinda's live-in boyfriend of three years, Jim, had recently hit her across the face. She now sported a big black eye, which she was unsuccessfully trying to mask with make-up. Unbelievably, Lucinda blamed herself: "He's pissed off at me 'cause I can't find a job. He says he's sick of carrying all the weight, so he wanted to get it through to me how much pressure he's under. I know he never would have hit me if I'd find a job."

To calm Jim's fiery temper, Lucinda would prepare elaborate meals and desserts. The only problem was, Lucinda would end up consuming most of the food. It turned out that she was compulsively overeating to quell her tension and anxiety over her unemployment situation.

— Sixteen-year-old Lisa's boyfriend Frank never hit her—at least, not with his fists. Frank's weapon of choice was words. A very controlling and jealous young man, Frank was constantly accusing Lisa of cheating on him. If Lisa visited a girlfriend, Frank would call two or three times to check up on her whereabouts. Afterwards, he would suspiciously question her about the possible presence of other guys at her girlfriend's house.

As a result, Lisa lived in perpetual fear that she'd trigger a jealous rage in Frank. Lisa, like so many women, was taking responsibility for Frank's behavior and bad moods.

When I asked her what she was getting out of this relationship, Lisa would explain that Frank's jealousy proved just how much he loved her.

Lisa's weight was a direct result of the turmoil in her relationship. She was determined to lose 15 pounds, but as soon as her weight started dropping and her figure began to shape up, Frank would go crazy with suspicion and jealousy. "He's sure I'm trying to lose weight to attract another boyfriend," Lisa complained.

— Connie's boyfriend Tim was committing the ultimate abusive and manipulative act: He was always threatening to commit suicide if she ever left him. Any woman who has been on the receiving end of this type of emotional blackmail experiences enormous feelings of responsibility and guilt. She feels trapped in the relationship, fearing that her boyfriend will kill himself if she leaves and that she'd never be able to forgive herself if that happened.

One night after Connie tried to break up with Tim, he locked himself in his car and put a gun to his head while Connie stood helplessly outside the car. "I'm gonna do it! I'm gonna shoot myself!" Tim kept taunting. "It'll be all your fault, too!" Connie was beside herself with panic and horror.

The weight of this pressure led her to regularly binge on high-fat foods. Somehow, when Connie was eating a cheeseburger, she didn't feel quite so bad about Tim. After she'd gained 20 pounds, she decided to remain with Tim, rationalizing that she was fortunate that he didn't criticize her extra weight.

Date and Acquaintance Rape

Most women discover at a very tender age that young men are unusually interested in sex. In most cases, she first discovers this truth when a date is coming to an end, and her companion sticks his hand under her blouse. At that point, she must grapple with the questions most women deal with while growing up: How far do I let him go? If I give in, will he lose all respect for me? If I don't give him what he wants, will he dump me for some girl who will?

For the guy, the question is usually answered without much hesitation: Yes, give me sex. Now! For the girl, the dilemma is much more complicated and can result in serious consequences. *She's* the one who would get pregnant. *She's* the one who would get a bad reputation. *She's* the one who stands to lose him if she says no.

— Sixteen-year-old Sandra was on her first date with Matt, a popular quarterback on the high school football team. On the way home from the movie they had just seen, Matt drove his car to a secluded spot, and the two of them made out passionately. Sandra, a virgin, enjoyed Matt's kisses and the feel of his muscular arms around her body. But when he reached up under her skirt, Sandra protested.

"Come on, Sandra," he said in response to her hesitation. "I want you so much. Don't be a tease." Sandra pushed his hand off her legs, but Matt's grip just tightened all the more. Sandra tried with all her might to pull away, but she was no match for the determined athlete. He pushed her skirt up and, while pinning down Sandra's upper body with his own torso, Matt forcibly stuck his fingers into her vagina.

"Ouch!" Sandra started yelling at the top of her lungs. "Stop! You're hurting me!"

Since he couldn't stifle her screams, Matt angrily lifted himself off of Sandra's squirming body. "Get out!" he ordered, shoving her out the car door. Then he drove off with tires squealing, leaving Sandra to walk the two miles back home in the dark.

The next morning at school, several kids looked at Sandra with funny expressions. In fact, she noticed that people were treating her differently all day, some giggling as she walked by, others avoiding making eye contact with her.

Matt hadn't wasted time spreading ugly rumors, which quickly circulated throughout the school, that he had "done her" the night before. He embellished the story further, making Sandra sound "easy" and promiscuous. Now, her peers were ostracizing her.

During the months that followed, Sandra became increasingly isolated from her classmates. She walked home alone, and she rarely left the house on weekends. Instead, she turned to food for comfort and companionship, and gained 15 pounds by the end of her junior year.

Date rape (or attempted date rape) is a common occurrence among adult women, as well. My client Janice's date, Gus, had nonconsensual sex with her after she passed out from a night of drinking too much wine. She blamed herself for her alcohol overconsumption, but that didn't prevent Janice from manifesting symptoms of "Rape Syndrome."

She became depressed and started overeating and oversleeping. She isolated herself from her friends, and neglected her normal grooming and housecleaning habits. Janice became so suspicious of the men that she'd meet that she wouldn't accept any dates—even when the person asking her out was someone she knew.

As is the case with date rape survivors such as those mentioned above, acquaintance rape victims comprise another segment of the female population that often indulges in self-blame for an act that was perpetrated upon them without their volition. These women tend to turn their anger away from the perpetrator and toward themselves, most often resulting in depression and a marked lack of self-esteem.

— Lynne was moving out of her apartment when the man who lived across the hall asked if she needed help. She gratefully accepted his offer, saying that she could use some assistance carting a large box of dishes down to her car. The man entered her apartment, closed the door, and then forcibly raped her.

Lynne never called the police, figuring they'd blame her "for having the stupidity to invite a near-stranger into my apartment." She suffered tremendous guilt and mentally berated herself for being "so stupid." Two months later, she quit her job and returned to her hometown to live with her parents.

Feeling like a helpless, incompetent little girl, Lynne readily returned to her girlhood eating habits. She binged on her mother's home-cooked meals and desserts and abandoned the exercise regimen she had established over the years. By the time she started therapy, Lynne was convinced that she had lost the capacity to achieve anything of value in life.

The Ultimate Violation: Rape by a Stranger

When a woman is forced to submit to sexual intercourse, it is called *rape*. Usually, this act of violence occurs without warning, and the victim is not only hurt physically, but is terrorized psychologically, as well. The rapist's sick fantasy often involves punishing a woman for the perceived crimes of other females he's been involved with—his mother, ex-wife, or girlfriend. He may have reached the point where his only means of pleasure or sexual gratification is through humiliating and controlling his female victim. Bottom line: The rape has little to do with sex, and everything to do with power.

In addition to the vicious act of rape itself, the perpetrator may verbally assault his victim with foul epithets, force her to engage in revolting acts such as eating excrement, and make her believe that he will kill her if she does not submit to him. So, in the midst of one of the most degrading and nightmarish experiences of this victim's life, she is also coping with the fear of death.

Rapists often use weapons such as knives or hammers, which leave permanent scars on their victims. One woman I worked with had her skull bashed in and had to undergo many reconstructive surgeries. Another woman had her hair hacked off during a gang rape.

The victim is humiliated. She is horrified. She wants to disappear.

The post-traumatic shock disorder accompanying the act of rape leaves a variety of symptoms in its wake, including:

- Sleep disorders: insomnia, oversleeping, night terrors and sweats, repeated nightmares about the attack

- Feelings of jumpiness and insecurity; agoraphobia

- Abuse of alcohol, drugs, or food.

- Sexual disorders, encompassing both a lack of desire for sex or extreme promiscuity

- Relationship difficulties: being irritable, argumentative, defensive, isolative, secretive, and exhibiting wide mood swings with one's partner

- Involuntarily reliving the experience

In light of the many problems that must be dealt with, most rape survivors derive beneficial results from treatment with a knowledgeable therapist, who will point out that a great deal of the pain that they are experiencing is tied in to two issues:

1. Feeling a lack of control over their personal safety.

2. Blaming themselves. This is really an attempt to regain a feeling of control. "If only I hadn't walked down that street," etc., is a way for the victim to reassure herself that if she takes the proper precautions from now on, she will be safe.

One study conducted a few years back (Bownes, I. T., 1990) found that in a sample of 51 rape survivors, 70 percent exhibited symptoms of post-traumatic stress disorder, which made them especially prone to anxiety and depression.

Some of the rape survivors I've worked with were also guilt-ridden with respect to the response they had as a result of penile penetration: vaginal lubrication. Incest and rape survivors alike secretly chastise themselves for this normal physiological reaction. What they learn in therapy is that just because the body may have responded to the rape or incest with certain feelings (some involving pleasure), it doesn't mean that they themselves actually enjoyed the act. The vagina lubricates itself in response to any stimulation—an involuntary reflex that is out of the victim's control. So, she learns to focus on the more crucial issues: the physical pain involved, the violation of her rights, the nonconsensual sex, and so on. She didn't ask for, or in any way do something to cause, the act of rape or incest, and she needs to stop blaming herself.

The shame that the victim feels is one of the FATS emotions—Fear, Anger, Tension, and Shame—that triggers the desire to overeat. As you read further, your healing will continue to unfold, so it's important to note that a chief ingredient in the healing process is turning shame and accompanying self-blame into positive feelings. As soon as you transform Fear, Anger, Tension, and Shame into Forgiveness, Acceptance, and Trust of Self, you can make the final leap to Forget All That Stuff, and then put the pain and the pounds behind you.

Fear
Anger
Tension
Shame

$\longrightarrow$

Forgiveness
Acceptance
Trust of
Self

Forget
All
That
Stuff

RELEASING
YOUR
POUNDS
OF PAIN

REMEMBERING AND
RELEASING THE PAIN

*"Courage is resistance to fear, mastery of fear—
not absence of fear."*
                                        —Mark Twain

YOU'VE NOW READ about many different types of people who have put on pounds of pain as a result of various traumatic situations. Maybe you've seen yourself portrayed in several of the case studies; perhaps only one or two struck a chord. I've offered some degree of therapeutic guidance throughout this book so far, but it probably still feels as if the pain and excess pounds are here to stay.

In this chapter, and those that follow, I'll help you do the ground-work necessary to completely release your pain, so you won't feel a need to hold on to your extra pounds.

Whose Fault Is It Anyway?

Children who experience emotional pain blame themselves. They are too young to understand that when someone else—especially a grown-up—commits a wrongful act, it is *that* person's fault and not their own. The closest that children come to blaming others is when they point the finger at a brother, sister, or peer. Children rarely, if ever, point the finger at Mom, Dad, or other adults.

Instead, the child is conditioned to think along these lines: "If Daddy is being this mean to me, he must be very angry. I must be a very bad girl to make Daddy this mad." If an abusive situation continues, the child's negative thinking progresses to an even greater extent: "If it's my fault that this horrible thing is happening, then I must be a horrible person."

As small children, we are not responsible for the bad things that happen to us. We are naturally irresponsible beings who don't know any better. We learn responsibility in three ways: by listening to the lessons taught to us by our parents and other authority figures, by modeling the responsible behavior we see in our parents and others, and by learning the hard way through trial and error. All these methods take time; we don't actually have a firm grasp on the "rules" until we are older children.

However, as soon as we do begin to differentiate between right and wrong, we (if we're basically well-behaved kids) follow our parents' rules because it feels so good to get their approval, and it feels so bad to incur their disapproval. We still don't fully comprehend the rationale behind the rules; we only understand the consequences of not following them.

The onset of mature thinking is evinced when the older child or adolescent starts to "take the role of the other." This means that the child is able to view the world through the other person's eyes. The child can imagine how someone else feels and thinks—that is, she empathizes. At this stage, the child begins to understand that Mommy and Daddy aren't superhumans—they are simply human beings who experience joy, pain, confusion, and stress, just like anyone else. At this point in the child's development, she sees that the parent is capable of making a mistake or acting out of poor judgment.

It's also at this stage that many abuse survivors begin feeling sorry for their abusers. That's especially tragic, because it is absolutely essential for the abuse survivor to acknowledge one very important point when healing oneself from abuse: The adult was entirely responsible for the abusive act. And along with that acknowledgment and understanding comes the accompanying anger toward the perpetrator, as well as toward the act itself.

Repressed Pain, Forgotten Memories

By the time an abused child is six or seven, she may have experienced so much emotional neglect or psychological, physical, or sexual battery that she doesn't know any other way of life. Pain is normal to her. She may have even repressed the abuse. And while an abused adult has access to support groups, reading materials, and health professionals, a child in this situation has few resources to help her deal with trauma. She must rely on her wits, her imagination, and sheer intestinal fortitude to endure the pain. Many abuse survivors I've worked with have actually learned to split their awareness in two during an abusive incident.

My client Rebecca, for example, remembers being beaten by her parents. She would curl herself up into a fetal position and try to will herself to disappear during the beatings. Sometimes she imagined that she was leaving her body and that her soul was up on the ceiling, watching her father whipping her body. That was her way of dealing with incomprehensible pain.

Many children enter into this state of splitting off from reality, or *dissociation*. The word literally means *dis-associating yourself* from the situation. For children, dissociating may be their only escape route from abuse, and it often evolves into a routine coping mechanism as the child gets older.

Sometimes, painful childhood memories are repressed so deeply that the adult survivor honestly doesn't remember any of the abuse. At least, she doesn't consciously remember. Now, this would be an acceptable state of affairs if the underlying symptoms of abuse weren't so disruptive. If the abuse survivor grew up with a healthy body and mind, enjoying full and satisfying interpersonal relationships, then I'd be the first person to say that it's just as well she doesn't remember the horror she's gone through. Why dwell on such pain unless it serves some useful purpose?

Unfortunately, most survivors—whether they've forgotten the abuse or not—have a lava pit of anger bubbling deep within them. This anger manifests itself in chronic health problems such as cancer, gynecological disorders, back or neck pain, migraines, hemorrhoids, heart palpitations, skin problems, insomnia, alcoholism, and obesity. The abuse survivor usually doesn't have a very happy adult life. She probably has difficulties maintaining relationships, and she may hate her job.

But worst of all, she may hate herself. As an outgrowth of this self-loathing, she ends up neglecting her physical health. She overeats and avoids exercise because she doesn't believe that she deserves to have an attractive body. Other people are worthy of beauty; other people deserve good. Not me. I'm bad.

That is why she *must* remember the abuse. She must remember so she can tell her inner child—the little girl living inside her—that she isn't to blame for the bad things that happened. She must hug that little girl and explain that the perpetrator was the one responsible for the abuse.

This news will make the little girl angry. Very, very angry. After all, it's an injustice to harm a little child! How could someone have dared hurt her!

It is when she has finally come to this realization that the anger—and most of the pain—will be released.

False Memories?

As I've discussed in earlier chapters, a lot of the afternoon talk shows are featuring "therapists" who say that it's not possible to completely repress memories of abuse. Well, I know from my dealings with thousands of abuse survivors that repression *is* an extremely common coping mechanism.

However, many women do not remember the abuse they experienced until a dramatic life event occurs. My client Tracy had completely pushed the memory of incest out of her conscious awareness. If you'd asked her, she would have sworn that she'd had an ideal home life, with perfect parents. As I stated before, though, people who insist that everything was "perfect" while growing up are often abuse survivors who are overcompensating in order to keep a tight lid on an unexamined and painful childhood. It's a "No, I won't look at it! I can't bear to look!" syndrome.

Tracy's memories of being molested and being the victim of forced oral sex didn't surface until she'd given birth to a little girl of her own—a phenomenon that is very common. A woman often does not recall her own girlhood trauma until she has a baby girl. She tends to "see" herself in this little girl, and then usually remembers the traumatic incident.

It is true that an inexperienced or overly zealous therapist can convince someone she was abused, even if she wasn't. I've seen this happen, and the results can rip families apart. But even in these "false memory" cases, something's going on there with the patient who claims to have remembered the abuse. She must have experienced some sort of emotional distress or parental neglect, or a therapist wouldn't be able to wield such power over her in the first place. Somewhere in the past, she learned to relinquish control.

Now, why would people want to identify themselves as abuse survivors unless something had actually happened? Well, if they need an "identity" that much, then something is sorely missing from their lives.

It's a little like the case of some men I saw in psychotherapy many years ago who were posing as Vietnam vets suffering from post-traumatic stress disorder. These men had never served in Vietnam, yet they had recounted graphically detailed war stories for me and the rest of the psychiatric hospital staff. One man burst into tears as he described his buddy's body being blown up in front of him. Later, when the staff discovered that these men were posing as vets, we were all understandably upset and confused.

However, we were all certain of one fact: Even if these men didn't suffer from post-traumatic stress disorder from the war, they were definitely sick and in need of help. Why else would they embrace such a dramatic identity? Why did they need so much attention? Psychiatric attention at that.

Well, I believe "false memory incest survivors" are in similar straits. They may not have actually experienced incest, but there is definitely something wrong—some pain somewhere is triggering their cry for help. I think that instead of criticizing and dismissing them, we need to focus on helping them.

Most Don't Forget

Most abuse survivors don't repress or forget their painful pasts. Instead, they minimize what happened. In essence, they shrug their shoulders and say, "Yes, this happened, but so what? It's over, and there's nothing I can do to change that now."

True. The past is the past. But, if you're chronically overeating, that's a clear signal that the past is haunting you now. So, *now* is the time to take care of it. You could wait for a better, less hectic time in your life to confront your "ghosts," but that time will never arrive, will it? There will never be complete tranquility in your life—not until you address these issues, anyway.

Many abuse survivors minimize their painful pasts by downplaying how bad it was. "Yes, my brother molested me, but I'm strong so it didn't bother me as much as it could have," or "It's true that he forced me to have sex, but I can deal with it," or "It wasn't that bad; I don't want to dwell on it."

This type of minimization is just one more defense mechanism shielding the survivor from pain. If you decide "it's not that bad," then you won't feel as if you'll explode from the rage. You won't "go crazy" wondering, Why me? Why me?

Also, if you've lived with this memory for 10, 20, 30 years or more, it becomes old news in your mind. You've lived with the pain so long, it seems to be a part of you. *But just because you're used to it, that doesn't mean it hasn't affected you.* Those are two separate issues.

I'm asking you now, to briefly re-experience the pain you endured as a child. I know that if you do that you'll walk through a "wall" within yourself. And beyond that wall lies greater peace of mind, the ability to love and relax, and a reduction in your appetite for food. Please trust that my years of working with abuse survivors has taught me that if you allow yourself to face this pain, you will lift the veil that is darkening your spirits.

You see, your natural, normal state is a being that experiences happiness and joy. God created you so you could enjoy life and feel pleasure. He wants you to feel free and happy as you go through your daily activities, not bogged down with guilt and frustration.

Your true self is light in body and spirit. Why not release it by summoning up the courage to slay the dragon of your past. What have you got to lose but the misery and the pounds?

Feel the Feelings

THE TRUE YOU IS LIGHT
IN BODY AND SPIRIT

*"Faith is to believe what we do not see; and the
reward of this faith is to see what we believe."*
—St. Augustine

YOUR TRUE BEING, the way God created you, is someone who feels
safe, secure, and happy. The true inner you is a free-spirited and loving little girl who embraces life and rejoices in its pleasures. She is
thoughtful and giving, both to others and herself. She balances duty
and play and doesn't feel guilty about relaxing and recharging her
batteries.

As we've seen, the essence of this true being gets distorted by childhood pain and abuse. The immature child blames herself for this abuse
and turns the anger—which rightfully belongs to the abuser—on herself. She eats to cover up the pain, as well as to punish herself for being
"unworthy and bad." But the true being is still there, deep inside. She
never leaves because she was originally created mentally and physically healthy. She has simply become distorted, like a child seeing herself in a funhouse mirror.

Four primary emotions are products of this distortion, emotions that
trigger overeating episodes in female abuse survivors. They are Fear,
Anger, Tension, and Shame—our FATS feelings that make us fat!

However, it always seems that we're more aware of the hunger for
food than we are of the emotions that trigger it. It's very common for
abuse survivors to be out of touch with their feelings, opinions, and
body sensations.

For example, my client Monica swore she was never angry even though she was always clenching her jaw and fists. Another client, Suzanne, had adapted to her explosively abusive household by being super-agreeable to everyone. She had no idea what her own opinions were on politics, abortion, religion, or anything of consequence (even whether she enjoyed a movie or not); she was too afraid of offending someone and risking an outburst of anger. Still another client, Rosie, was not aware that her too-tight shoes, clothing, and bra were pinching and hurting her. She had learned—from years of abuse— how to turn off her awareness of pain and discomfort.

These clients, and others I've worked with, were frustrated by psychologists and self-help books that implored them to "get in touch with their feelings." But Monica, Suzanne, Rosie, and other abuse survivors had no idea what a "feeling" was, in the first place! Yes, perhaps they caught glimpses of feelings such as empathy for others, guilt, frustration, subdued anger, and tepid romantic love. But, for the most part, their access to the normal wide range of human emotions had been distorted and blunted.

I have found that the best way to begin working with an abuse survivor is to start with the basics. So, if you have been a victim of abuse, I'm going to ask you at this very moment to become aware of the sensation of your body sitting on your chair. Notice how your back feels against the chair, and how your bottom feels. Does the chair feel hard or cushiony? Warm or cool? Is the fabric scratchy or soft?

How about your feet? Are they relaxed? Are your shoes tight and stiff, or flexible and light? Are your feet too cold, warm, or just right?

What about your clothing? Is your bra confining you in any way? How about your underwear, including your panty hose or stockings? Is the waistband of your pants, skirt, or dress comfortable? Does it bind at all, or is it okay as is?

Where are your hands right now? Does their position signal relaxation or tension? How about your jaw—is it tight or sore in any way? Or is it relaxed?

Becoming aware of the sensations in each part of your body is an important first step in recognizing and acknowledging the other parts of your true being.

Recognizing Your FATS Signals

What's the difference between normal physical hunger and the hunger brought on by Fear, Anger, Tension, and Shame? Since it takes time to learn how to recognize FATS feelings, here's a good clue: Physical hunger is gradual, while <u>emotional hunger happens instantly.</u>

With physical hunger, your body will give you slowly evolving signals that it wants to eat. First, you'll feel a little gnawing in your stomach. Then, you'll notice a slight hunger pang, and your stomach may growl with emptiness. Eventually, you'll be driven to eat out of necessity.

With emotional hunger—triggered by the FATS feelings—your hunger suddenly speeds up from 0 to 100 miles an hour. One minute, you're not even thinking about food. The next, you're starving! This isn't physical hunger; it's definitely emotional.

Emotions are relayed to awareness in much the same manner that radio signals are. If we have our "radio"—that is, our awareness of our emotions—tuned in to the right frequency, we'll know exactly what we're feeling most of the time. Many abuse survivors learn at a very young age that survival depends on tuning in their "radios" to the adult abusers around them. They become exquisitely sensitive to the people in their world, as Dianne was.

> — Dianne never knew when her alcoholic father's temper would explode, so she learned to tune in to his moods. In this way, she could feel some semblance of control in an otherwise chaotic situation. Dianne tuned out her own feelings of fear, and tuned in her father's "frequency" so she could anticipate his behavior. This was the "system" she used in order to avoid beatings.
>
> As an adult, Dianne's radio was still tuned off of her own

frequency. She was one of the sweetest people you'd ever want to meet, but at 225 pounds, she wasn't really very happy with herself. Dianne's early childhood survival mechanism had turned her into a major people-pleaser, a woman afraid of listening to her own feelings.

The first "fattening" feeling that Dianne and I worked on in therapy was:

Fear

Overeating in response to fear is very normal because of the calming effect of food. Overeating episodes are triggered by many different manifestations of fear:

- *Insecurity.* Feeling that you're unqualified, don't deserve good things, or that you don't fit in; feeling fat in clothing; feeling like an "impostor" or a fake; feeling unprepared for an important event such as a presentation, speech, test, or job interview.

- *Walking on eggshells.* Fear that your bad-tempered spouse, boss, parent, etc., will explode if you say or do something wrong; fear that you'll lose your job for the slightest dereliction of duty.

- *Generalized fear.* A feeling of impending doom; fear that if something good happens, then bad is sure to follow (as if there's a cause-and-effect relationship); overwhelming and unrealistic fears of trauma, such as being murdered, burning in a fire, being killed in an accident, etc.; jittery nervousness triggered by post-traumatic stress.

- *Abandonment fears.* Constant fear that your lover or spouse will leave you or cheat on you; fear that your friends don't like you; fear that your parents will die; fear of being alone.

- *Existential fears.* Fear that your life has no meaning or purpose; fear that you're "missing the boat" or opportunities; fear that you are a "nothing" or a hollow being.

- *Control issues.* Fear that others are trying to control you; fear of authority figures; fear of taking responsibility for yourself; phobias connected to driving a car or being in an airplane; fear of being vulnerable and getting hurt; fear of commitment and/or marriage.

- *Sexual fears.* Fear of the opposite sex in general; fear of receiving attention from, or talking to, the opposite sex; fear of sexual relations; fear of looking attractive.

- *Intimacy fears.* Fear of showing your true colors (they might reject or hurt the real you); fear of getting close to someone (this person might abandon you).

In chapter 11, you'll read about some of the methods that my clients employ to overcome Fear and the other FATS feelings. For now, let's continue recognizing the emotions that trigger an excessive appetite for food.

Anger

There is nothing inherently wrong with anger. Yet, it is the number one emotion triggering compulsive overeating, especially in women. Much of our training as young girls teaches us to minimize, downplay, and disguise our feelings of anger—after all, it's not "ladylike" to scream and yell, is it?

But, anger is a normal emotion in response to a perceived wrong. We are angry when we are born, due to the trauma of birth. We are angry as babies when we feel hungry, thirsty, wet, or tired. As children, we feel anger toward classmates who hit us, or little brothers who steal our toys.

However, as adolescents, the social pressure to "act like a lady" starts taking grip, and we begin to turn the anger inward. Instead of being angry at the stupid system of choosing kids for school sports teams during gym class, we feel sad when we're chosen last. We feel ugly when our first boyfriend breaks up with us. We feel humiliated when the popular kids poke fun at us. We blame ourselves for wrongs and feel depressed, instead of expressing anger outwardly. Is it any wonder that in adolescence, girls' self-esteem drops way below the level of boys'?

Abuse survivors blame themselves for the incest and molestation that occurred in their past, and rape survivors blame themselves, as well. However, when we reach adulthood, anger is often no easier to deal with or admit to than when we were children. Take Martha, for example.

— As a customer service representative for a major department store, Martha received returned merchandise and gave refunds or store credit all day long. Many customers were aggressive and would make outrageous requests, such as asking for full refunds for old, broken merchandise. Martha had no outlet for the anger that this behavior inspired, so she would come home at night feeling drained and hungry. She'd head right to the refrigerator and eat whatever was quick and filling: ice cream, cookie dough, any type of leftovers. It didn't matter what type of food it was as long as it could be consumed quickly and easily. Martha was vainly attempting to quell the boiling cauldron of anger deep within her by filling it with food.

— Another client, Jan, was quite cognizant of the anger residing within her when she entered therapy. However, she expressed her trepidation about releasing this anger for fear that she'd completely lose control. The poised, well-dressed woman told me, "I just know that if I let out this anger, I'll do something radical like smash down all the walls in my house or break things."

Years and years of repressed anger had been stopped up by a 50-pound layer of fat on her body. But, as Jan let out her steam bit by bit over the months, she was able to maintain control of her emotions. And as the steam of anger was released, so too were the pounds and overactive appetite.

Throughout this book, I discuss healthy and effective ways to handle and reduce feelings of anger. A 1994 study by University of Tennessee's Sandra Thomas, Ph.D., R.N., also lends help in this area. In a survey of 535 women, Thomas found that women who held in their anger and tried to deny that it existed were besieged by physical problems such as headaches and upset stomachs. Women who vented anger by yelling or slamming doors also were prone to body aches and pains. Thomas concluded that both methods—suppressing anger and violently venting anger—increase the actual rage we feel inside. This increased rage then leads to physical problems. Interestingly enough, and perhaps most important, is that both groups exhibited very low self-esteem.

Thomas found that women with the fewest (or without any) health problems, and with the highest self-esteem, handled anger in healthier ways. These included cathartic activities such as exercise, journal writing, or talking to a supportive person; having a reasonable and calm discussion with the person who instigated the anger; and using negotiating principles to solve problems.

Tension

Tension is the physical manifestation of stress. Stress itself really doesn't hurt us, because it is caused by forces outside of our beings. It is our *internalization* of the stress, in the form of tension and anxiety, that is the problem. "Stress management" has always seemed to be a contradictory term to me, because we can't control the stress in the world; we can only control or manage our internal response to stress: tension. Trying to control something uncontrollable, such as stress, only creates more tension. Besides, a lot of stressful situations result in positive outcomes, such as buying a home, celebrating the holidays, and getting married. In addition, what causes tension in some people does not cause it in others. Our beliefs about, and interpretation of, a situation are what cause tension in our bodies, and also determine the *amount* of tension we experience.

The renowned philosopher and author, Rollo May, argues against using the word *stress* to describe both cause and effect—that is, he says it is a mistake to use *stress* synonymously with the word *anxiety* because the former is the cause and the latter is the effect. May writes, "If we use stress as a synonym for anxiety, we cannot distinguish between the different (underlying) emotions" such as fear, grief, and anger.

It is for this reason that I prefer to use the word *tension*, because this is the most identifiable outcome of stressors. The tension reaction leads to overeating, as we seek to relax and unwind with the comfort of ice cream, cookies, hamburgers, or even "health foods."

Tension is also a major factor leading to compulsive overeating due to psychological and physical forces. New studies point to brain chemistry changes in response to tension. These changes increase our craving for certain foods, especially those loaded with carbohydrates. A high-carbohydrate diet can be healthful, but only if composed of low-fat foods eaten in moderation. Tension often triggers the consumption of high-fat carbohydrates such as chocolate, cake, cookies, breads, or the binging on huge quantities of "fat-free" carbohydrates such as rice cakes or muffins.

Several well-conducted studies (Strober; Cattanach; Mynors-Wallis; and Terr) have looked at the connection between "stressful life events," including child abuse and overeating. These studies have concluded that people who binge-eat or who have clinically diagnosed eating disorders have experienced significantly more life traumas and "stressors" than people who don't binge-eat. The researchers have also

130 ða.

determined that eating is the chief tension-management tool used by these trauma survivors.

research

Dr. Sarah Leibowitz of Rockefeller University has studied the relationship between tension and brain chemistry for 10 years and has made some fascinating discoveries (Marano, 1993). Leibowitz identified brain and hormonal substances influencing our cravings for carbohydrates, one of which was *cortisol,* a hormone that the brain produces to anesthetize pain. Interestingly enough, Leibowitz found that the adrenal glands produce excess cortisol in response to tension. The cortisol then stimulates production of a brain chemical called *neuropeptide Y,* identified by Leibowitz as being a chief factor in turning our carbohydrate cravings on and off.

In other words, tension makes us crave carbohydrates. And if we consume excess carbohydrates, especially high-fat varieties, it is converted into body fat. Even worse, reports Leibowitz, these tension-induced chemicals also make the body hang on to the new body fat we produce. So tension not only creates an overactive appetite, it makes it more difficult to lose body fat!

Another researcher, Judith Wurtman of M.I.T., has written many journal articles and books on the relationship between the brain chemical *serotonin* and carbohydrate cravings. Serotonin is a "messenger" chemical (a neurotransmitter) that is largely responsible for affecting our emotions and energy levels. When serotonin levels are low, our energy level and mood will be, too. Wurtman found that carbohydrates trigger a chemical reaction that increases serotonin production.

Since tension depletes and lowers serotonin levels,when you are experiencing prolonged tension, your carbohydrate cravings may be increased. (There is further discussion about the relationship between food, chocolate, beverages, and serotonin in chapters 12 and 13.)

Another interesting study from Yale University found a disturbing relationship between tension and "pot-bellies" (Bricklin, M., 1993). Yale researchers Marielle Rebufe-Scrive, Ph.D., and Judith Rodin, Ph.D., concluded from extensive work with animal and human subjects that tension triggers chemical reactions in the body, which increases the amount of one's body fat, especially around the mid-section; and abdominal fat is associated with an increased risk for heart disease, stroke, and diabetes in both men and women.

In light of these facts, before I turn to a discussion of the final FATS feeling (shame), I'm going to discuss some ways to lower the health risks mentioned above.

❧ Three Ways to Stop Procrastinating and Start Exercising ❧

Exercise increases the amount of serotonin your brain produces (Chaouloff, F., et al., 1989), which lessens your carbohydrate cravings, elevates your energy level, and brightens your mood. Exercise is the best tension-management tool and body-fat burner there is, yet many of us resist it. Why?

I think it's due to some of the unrealistic expectations and myths perpetuated about exercise. First, there's this false notion that exercise is supposed to be fun. I don't know about you, but my idea of fun involves something a little more relaxing than huffing, puffing, and sweating. For most (not all) people, exercise is, at best, mildly enjoyable. Don't get me wrong—I'm a huge advocate of exercise, and I even work out five to six times a week. But is it fun? Come on, let's be honest here! I love *having* exercised, but I really don't love it while I'm doing it!

The second erroneous assumption concerning exercise is that you're supposed to do it at a gym. While this works for some people, I personally can't stand gyms. Especially aerobic classes. The minute I drive up to a gym, I feel tension. I can never find a parking space easily, and when I get into the gym, it's a loud, crowded place where the air is hot and sweaty and they're often playing really loud disco music. Not only that, but I also take exception to the *de rigueur* fashion show, the quasi-singles bar scene, and the overly complicated aerobic dance steps taught by a screaming dynamo.

Seriously, though, what I've learned is that exercise is only effective if you stick with it. And the only way to do so is if the particular form of exercise fits your personality. I am a person who needs lots of intellectual stimulation. I love reading and having great conversations. So, I found an exercise program that allowed me to read while working out: the Stairmaster! You can also read while pedaling on a stationary bicycle. Or, you can watch television while jogging on a treadmill.

I've learned how to trick myself into exercising, and it's worked well for the past five years. I still don't love to exercise, but then, I don't expect to. Here are the tricks that work well for me, which have also worked well for my clients and workshop attendees:

1. *See exercise as part of your daily routine, not something that is optional.* Why? Because when you ask yourself each day, "Do I exercise today, or don't I?," you might very well decide that you don't have enough time. Instead, you've got to go to the bank, the store, the office, just about anyplace where you can avoid exercising. The minute we allow ourselves to have the "will I or won't I" argument, we increase the odds that we won't exercise.

So, stop viewing exercise as an optional activity. It's not! It's a necessity for a long, healthy life (in conjunction with weight control and tension management, of course).

You might try writing down your exercise schedule in ink on your calendar, just as you do your other important appointments and meetings that you cannot miss. Figure out a realistic schedule for exercising several times a week, and then stick to it. Never cancel your exercise session; if something unavoidable comes up, simply reschedule your session within the same day.

2. *Pair exercise with something you enjoy.* This really works for me. I make sure I always have something interesting to read—a new magazine, a book, or an intriguing newspaper article. Then, I don't let myself read it unless I'm exercising. As I mentioned before, I get really bored exercising unless my mind is also being stimulated. My Stairmaster allows me the flexibility of reading while I'm working out strenuously (I work out 45 minutes a day, 6 days a week, 5½ to 6 miles per workout). I've found that reading health-oriented magazines

such as *Prevention, Longevity, New Body*, and *Shape* are very motivational while working out.

Also, be patient with yourself if you're just starting to exercise. If you are overweight, I urge you to consider taking a class especially designed for people of a larger size. Most often, the instructors are women who have lost a great deal of weight and who understand the unique problems and challenges that a heavy person experiences. Therefore, the exercise routines are geared toward your special needs and limitations.

You'll find, especially in these classes geared toward larger women, that you'll be surrounded by a support system that is very inspirational. And you'll probably feel more comfortable wearing sweats or leotards around other women who are also trying to lose weight.

I also do a mini-weight workout every other day. Like most exercise, weight workouts are not my idea of great fun. But, the results are definitely worth it. Thanks to this weight training, my muscles feel more toned and shaped than they have in my whole life.

To motivate myself, I do my weight workouts while listening to my favorite radio talk show. If my schedule doesn't allow me to work out at that time, I tape the show and listen to it later. If I were working out at a gym or jogging somewhere, I'd take a cassette player with me.

Many of my clients pair television viewing with workouts on treadmills and stationary bicycles. If, for example, you videotape your favorite soap opera while you're at work every day, don't allow yourself to watch it unless you exercise.

I find it very interesting that a recent survey (Neergaard, 1993) showed that 64 percent of 1,018 sedentary Americans said that they would like to exercise but don't have enough time. In the same survey, 84 percent of these people reported watching at least three hours of television a week. The surveyors concluded, as you may have guessed, that the solution was to exercise while watching television.

3. *Do the "15-minute trick."* Here's another great motivator, especially for those days when you just don't want to exercise. Tell your-

self, "I'll only work out for 15 minutes. If I feel like stopping at the end of those 15 minutes, I will." Nine times out of ten, you'll keep going at the end of your allotted time. After all, you've already gone to the trouble of putting on your workout clothes and shoes. But, if you really want to stop after 15 minutes, allow yourself to do so.

Shame

Shame is the final FATS emotion that can trigger overeating. Shame is self-blame, guilt, self-doubt, depression, and low self-esteem all wrapped up in one. Think of the little dog who has been beaten, yelled at, and ignored. She keeps her head down low and her tail between her legs, sending a message that she hopes will protect her from further injury: "I'm not a threat, I'm weak. Please don't hurt me. I'm sad and I'm sorry."

I've worked with many clients who have exhibited these signs. Shame starts in childhood when the little girl blames herself for the neglect or abuse she receives. Instead of being angry at the abuser, she assumes that she must have caused the adult to be angry. She internalizes the anger, turning it toward herself instead of toward its rightful owner.

Since she blames herself, she feels guilt and shame. Sexual abuse and rape survivors often mentally beat themselves up for "causing" the incident, a lie perpetuated by the sexual offender who convinces her that she "asked for it." Her self-doubt ("Did I cause him to do this to me?") is further compounded by shame over any normal physical reactions of sexual arousal. She is horrified that her body would betray her like this!

Sexual abuse survivors usually feel damaged or broken. My client, Corrine, who was repeatedly raped by her father, was shocked when she got pregnant in her early thirties. "Deep down, I thought my uterus and womb were broken by the abuse," she told me.

In a study of 500 adolescents, researchers Cavaiola and Schiff (1989) found that 150 of the teenagers had been physically or sexually abused. These 150 teens had significantly lower self-esteem levels compared to the nonabused teens, regardless of what type of abuse the teen had suffered.

Another study of 78 eating-disordered females (Oppenheimer, 1985) concluded, "Frequently, the sexually molested subject has feelings of inferiority or disgust about her own femininity and sexuality. These may come to be entangled with concern about her body weight, shape, and size."

Shame triggers eating for a number of reasons. The woman experiencing this emotion eats for comfort, companionship, and recreation because she avoids social situations that normally fill these human needs. She isolates herself from others, judging herself as unworthy. "No one would like me anyway," she may assume.

Sadly, as the woman gains weight, the shame increases. Researchers (Martin, et al. 1988) administered self-esteem tests to 550 girls between the ages of 14 and 16. They found strong correlations between weight and self-esteem, concluding that "as weight increased, self-esteem decreased."

When she eats so much that her body becomes morbidly obese, the woman finds that people treat her fat body with contempt.

"I'll be out shopping and someone will say, 'What a fat pig' to me," said my client, Jody. "Do they think that just because I'm fat, I don't have any feelings?" Jody finds that she eats more on days when people are cruel to her.

Turning FATS Around

We've looked at different situations and feelings that trigger the appetite for food. We've also touched on several solutions. At this point, our goal is to become more aware and honest with ourselves.

When you're hungry, it's vital that you resist the impulse to automatically reach for food. Instead, ask yourself: "Could I be feeling Fear, Anger, Tension, or Shame?" Just by asking yourself that question, you'll feel more in control of your eating. In fact, in many instances, this question can eliminate the emotional hunger or, at least, reduce it to a controllable size.

The affirmations and visualization tools in the next chapter are the same ones I've used in my own healing, as well as with my clients and workshop attendees. Please take the time to put my suggestions into action. They really do work, but first you have to make the effort to implement them into your life! There is no easier way to permanently lessen your appetite for food—no magic pill, powder, or food combination.

BREAKING THE POUND/PAIN CYCLE

"So Jesus said to them because you have so lit-tle faith, I tell you the truth. If you have faith as small as a mustard seed, you can say to this mountain, 'Move from here to there' and it will move. Nothing will be impossible for you."
—*Matthew* 17:20

YOU'VE COME SO FAR already, and the best is yet to come. By changing your thinking, you will find that your body is changing. That means that your appetite will lessen, and your body fat will fall away. You will no longer need the defenses that food and fat give you—like the boundary that once separated East and West Germany. It's time to tear down your walls and lay down your weapons. You're no longer in danger; you are safe.

As a child, you were not responsible for what happened to you—the adult who harmed you was at fault. (As you've probably noticed, this is a point that I have never tired of making throughout this book.) So, the first thing I'd like you to do is call up a clear mental picture of yourself as a little girl or adolescent, around the time that you were first abused, neglected, injured, or hurt.

Now, please give that little girl a big mental hug. Tell her that it's okay, that it wasn't her fault, that you love her. Tell her not to worry. Most of all, tell her to forgive herself, since she didn't do any-thing wrong.

Whenever you feel the first FATS feeling, "Fear," I want you to immediately hug that little girl deep inside you. Tell her she's safe. Tell her you care.

Now you're starting to transform the FATS feelings from Fear, Anger, Tension, and Shame into Forgiving, Accepting, and Trusting one's Self. By giving your inner little girl lots of hugs, praise, encouragement, and love, you are essentially "re-parenting" yourself. You are being the mother and father that you needed when you were growing up. Think about the following aphorism, because I believe that it really hits the mark: "It's never too late to have a happy childhood."

Whenever you feel Fear, Anger, Tension, or Shame, immediately declare this affirmation: *"I Forgive, Accept, and Trust my Self."* Say it over and over, allowing the strength of the conviction to conquer feelings of insecurity.

That statement is the most important concept behind your healing—the phrase that will allow you to release your pounds of pain. Please write it down on a piece of paper or index card, and look at it often. You may want to tape the card to your bathroom mirror, refrigerator door, or car dashboard; or put it on your desk at work.

What follows are additional affirmations to use as part of your healing. In chapter 3, I described how I used these affirmations to heal the pain in my own life and how my clients made affirmation tapes to achieve remarkable accomplishments. I urge you to do the same.

❧ Affirmations ❧

I am a good person.
Today, I release my pain.
Right now, good is happening to me.
I love the little girl inside of me.
I am made in the image and likeness of God.
I take very good care of myself.
I deserve the best that life has to offer.
I am whole and complete.
I give myself permission to take care of my needs.

I enjoy taking care of myself.
God intends for me to be happy.
My family benefits when I'm happy.
I ask for, and accept, help from others.
I am strong.
I believe in my dreams.
I can achieve whatever I can see.
Today, I am taking steps toward realizing my dreams.
If it's going to be, it's up to me.
I accept challenges.
I am creative.
I am a good problem-solver.
I have common sense.
I am a successful person.
I take good care of my finances.
I surround myself with loving people.
I expect, and deserve, good relationships.
I attract happy, healthy people.
I am investing in my future.
It feels good to take care of myself.
I reward myself for my efforts.
This is the perfect time to work toward my dreams.
I trust my judgment and inner voice.
I am intuitive.
I sense the best path to follow.
I follow the path that is best for me.
I express my feelings.
It's okay for me to be honest.
I am always in good company.
I am safe and secure.
I expect the best to happen.
Good things are happening to me right now.
I am planting seeds for my future.
I enjoy my successes.
I accept compliments.

I take calculated risks.
It's okay to express my terms and conditions.
I am making a wish list, and it is being fulfilled.
All my dreams are coming true.
I am fulfilled in all aspects of my life.
All my needs are being met.
My body is perfect, healthy, and whole.

In her classic, inspirational book, *You Can Heal Your Life,* Louise Hay discusses the power of affirmations as one attempts to release addictions to food and cigarettes, as well as health or money problems. She writes:

> *I say to clients, "There must be a need in you for this condition, or you wouldn't have it. Let's go back a step and work on the WILLINGNESS TO RELEASE THE NEED. When the need is gone, you will have no desire for the cigarette or the overeating or the negative pattern.*
>
> *"One of the first affirmations to use is: I am willing to release the NEED for the resistance, or the headache, or the constipation, or the excess weight, or the lack of money or whatever. Say: 'I am willing to release the need for . . .' If you are resisting at this point, then your other affirmations cannot work."*

I heartily agree with Louise Hay's contention that when you feel the overwhelming urge to binge-eat, it's important to look underneath the urge and examine the motives driving you to this hunger. Instead of heading to the cupboard or refrigerator, pause one brief moment to ask yourself, "Am I running away from a troubling thought or emotion?" Just by posing this question, you'll regain enough awareness or composure to put the brakes on a potential binge situation before it accelerates.

The Power of Visualization

I've always been an advocate of the power of visualization and have used it to achieve incredible success in my own life. However, I don't think that visualization works as a result of any magic or divine intervention; rather, I believe that it's effective because, if you can picture yourself achieving a goal, you'll keep working toward it until you actually do so.

Before I was a published author, I visualized my book appearing in print. My mental image of my published book was graphically detailed; I even decided that Bantam, a major book publisher, would buy my manuscript. To make my visualization as real as possible, I cut the little Bantam logo—a rooster—off of the pages and covers of every Bantam paperback I owned. I taped these little roosters all around my house: on my bathroom mirror, on the refrigerator door, and everywhere else I could think of. During my daily meditations, I could picture my book in the bookstore with my name printed on the book spine, right below the Bantam rooster.

I hung on to this image until it felt like second nature to me. I trusted that if I worked hard enough, I would be published by Bantam, just as I had envisioned. Well, my first book, *My Kids Don't Live with Me Anymore: Coping with the Custody Crisis,* was almost bought by Bantam, but they decided at the last minute that since they already had a book on child custody in publication, they would pass on my project.

My second book was sold by auction through my literary agent, and Bantam was one of the publishers making a bid. Alas, they bid much lower than Harper & Row, who ended up publishing my second book, *The Yo-Yo Syndrome Diet.*

The third time was the charm, however. During my book tour for *The Yo-Yo Syndrome Diet,* most of the talk-show hosts and studio audience members wanted to discuss chocolate and chocoholism. My philosophy about chocoholism is two-fold: chocolate cravings stem from an unbalanced diet and/or psychological issues (many of which are addressed in this book); and second, if you totally abstain from chocolate, you'll feel deprived and end up indulging in a chocolate-eating binge. What's better is to eat a small amount of low-fat chocolate in moderation. That was a topic I'd covered only briefly in the book, so I decided to write a third book, *The Chocoholic's Dream Diet.*

Bantam was the first bidder on that book, and I jumped at the chance to be published by them! When the book came out, I saw it for the first time in a bookstore. There it was, just like I'd visualized it for four years, with my name on the book spine and the little red rooster right above it. That was a real thrill, and confirmed the power of visualization to me—I'd hung on to the picture in my mind until it came true!

One of the best books on the topic of visualization is *Positive Imaging* by Norman Vincent Peale. Actually, all of his books are wonderful, but this particular one is very focused on the visualization topic, and I've recommended it to many of my clients.

As I mentioned previously, I also found Louise Hay's *You Can Heal Your Life* extremely valuable in examining the destructive pictures that I held in my mind with respect to money and relationships. With the help of this book, I "edited" my images concerning my right to have financial and lovelife success. It helped me tremendously in achieving the fulfilling life that I have today.

See Yourself Thin: The Case of Elaine

Elaine was a woman who came to me for psychotherapy and also to lose weight. She was a sexy woman who took good care of her hair and face, and although her factory job required her to dress in jeans and T-shirts, she always looked well groomed. She told me during our first session that she was the only woman working in an otherwise all-male department.

Elaine, who stood 5'7" and weighed 235 pounds, had joined four weight-loss programs the year before she came to me. She easily lost weight with each dieting attempt but would always skid to a plateau as soon as she neared the 200-pound mark.

"I *never* get under 200 pounds," she firmly announced. Her words, as well as the inflection in her voice, told me that Elaine's weight plateau was a *decision* she'd made. But I didn't discuss this with her right away. She wouldn't have believed me.

Instead, Elaine participated in my traditional psychotherapy sessions with an emphasis on weight loss. It was no surprise to me that pounds started dropping off of her like fur shedding off a cat in the summer. Her weight went down to 230, 225, 220—down, down it went. Each week, we'd work on painful experiences from her present and her past—uncovering and releasing the pain, and along with it, the excess pounds.

Then it happened. She reached 202 pounds and stayed right there. For one-and-a-half months, her weight fluctuated between 201 and 204. Finally, when we both feared she'd abandon her weight-loss efforts altogether, I helped her acknowledge what she needed to see: Elaine couldn't get under 200 pounds because she couldn't *see* herself below that weight.

First, I asked Elaine to close her eyes to block out any distractions. I asked her to picture herself standing on her bathroom scale. We made the image vivid, and I asked her to describe everything she "saw" in her visualization. She described that she was wearing underwear, that her feet felt a little cold as she stepped on the metal scale, and that the toilet paper roll was almost empty.

Then I asked her to look at the number on the scale. What did it say? "202 pounds," she replied.

"Okay, I'd like you to picture that number changing. Can you imagine the scale saying 201?"

"Yes," said Elaine.

"Good. Now can you change the number to 200?"

After a moment, Elaine said, "Yes, it's 200 now."

"All right. Now let's keep going. I'd like you to see 199 on the scale."

There was silence.

"Can you see 199 on the scale, Elaine?" I asked.

"Um . . . well, not really," Elaine struggled to explain. Her eyes were now open wide as she told me, "Every time I see 199, it changes instantaneously back to 200!"

"Okay," I reassured her. "Let's try again. After you close your eyes, I'd like to ask you to take some really deep breaths. . . ."

We worked on her mental image for the remainder of our hour together. But it took another session before Elaine was able to see—and hold on to—an image of herself below 200 pounds. Once she was able to "lock on" to a firm, steady mental picture of the scale reaching 199, her actual weight followed suit. At the next week's session, Elaine hugged me and showed me a Polaroid snapshot she'd taken while standing on her bathroom scale. The photo revealed a pair of bare feet and red L.E.D. numbers blaring 199.

"Just like in our visualization!" Elaine exclaimed happily.

You see, until Elaine could actually visualize her weight below 200 pounds, she couldn't achieve that goal. She believed that she was destined to plateau at 200 pounds, and she unconsciously made this belief come true. Again, the power of visualization isn't the product of some voodoo magic—it just shows the impact that our decisions have on our lives.

Elaine had decided with absolute certainty that she could not get below 200 pounds. Every time she'd get close, she'd think, What's the use? and would slacken her weight loss efforts. She'd skip going to the gym. She'd use extra blue cheese salad dressing instead of the low-fat variety. And, sure enough, her weight would "plateau" as if by magic.

It didn't help that one of her diet club "counselors" (actually, an untrained salesperson wearing a white laboratory coat) had reinforced Elaine's belief in her 200-pound plateau. "It's your set-point," the counselor had told Elaine. "It's probably a genetically programmed weight that your body is comfortable with." That statement set into concrete Elaine's belief that she'd never reach her goal weight of 150 pounds.

A good analogy would be if someone was told her entire life, "You will never succeed, and you will never make anything of yourself."

Suppose that that person wanted to get a college degree, but held on to the belief that she'd always fail at any goal she attempted. If she finished all her college classes except for one, she'd be very close to her goal. But if she did not really believe that achieving that goal was possible (and didn't believe that she *deserved* to attain it), she would not allow herself to experience success. This is the kind of person who would suddenly find something "more important" to do—like get married, get a job, move away, or have a baby—and would seem to have a perfectly rational reason for falling short of reaching her goal. She would rationalize to herself and others why she couldn't complete her degree.

Elaine's adopted set-point theory—"I'm genetically programmed to have a weight plateau at 200 pounds"—was exactly the same thing. She'd get close to achieving her goal, and then would stop short. However, when I helped her change her mental picture, her expectations changed. And thus, we altered her behavior.

You Deserve to Have the Body You Desire

One of the barriers Elaine encountered was the sense that she didn't deserve to achieve her weight-loss goal. After her weight dropped down to about 180, Elaine began to fear that she'd put the weight back on. Why was this so? Since every extra pound on her body was equal to a pound of pain, we began exploring the issues that made her think she didn't deserve a normal-weight body.

As I mentioned before, Elaine's job thrust her into the middle of an all-male department. We discussed her feelings about male attention, and right away it was evident that this was an issue for Elaine. It turned out that she was afraid of men's admiring glances and compliments about her improved figure.

Elaine was one of those naturally sexy women who just oozed charisma and sex appeal, in spite of the excess weight she carried. She was like a Mae West with auburn hair—a woman with bedroom eyes and a throaty voice—and guys just went nuts for her. That fact petrified Elaine.

We discovered that she felt guilty about her natural power to attract men. To get to the root of this guilt, I asked Elaine to remember all the times she'd felt this way. Back, back, we went, uncovering layers of years when Elaine recalled that other women were jealous of her for getting all the boyfriends she wanted. Still, that wasn't the root of her guilt.

What we eventually uncovered stemmed from her childhood. Elaine and her father had had a close bond, and when they would go out on errands and day trips together, her father treated her like she was a grown-up. He'd talk to her about all sorts of things: his work, his dreams, and his girlfriends.

"His girlfriends?" I interrupted Elaine's recounting of her childhood. "But weren't your parents married for 40 years when he passed away?"

"Yes, but he had mistresses throughout their marriage. I don't know if Mom ever knew about the affairs, but Dad told me about each and every one of them," Elaine said with a grimace. "In fact, he used to take me along on his 'dates.' I guess I was his excuse to get out of the house."

Elaine and I discovered that, although she had been flattered to be Daddy's "special friend" and confidante, it was a burden she wasn't emotionally prepared to handle. She remembered that each girlfriend she met was always the same "type": voluptuous with a big hairdo. The three of them would eat at a restaurant, go to a movie, or go to the girlfriend's home. These women would then attempt to win Elaine's affection and approval, but she felt nothing but contempt and pity for them. They were, after all, threatening her mother's place in her life.

Elaine never told anyone about her father's affairs. When she grew up and found her own body mimicking the voluptuous figures of her Dad's girlfriends, Elaine was horrified. She was even more appalled when men began asking her out regularly. That's when she started putting the extra weight on.

Whenever Elaine's weight would drop at all, her naturally sexy figure and personality would begin to shine through. Men would start to notice her, and her guilt and fear would be triggered. She was especially aghast that most of the men at work were married, yet they would still make passes at her thinning body.

"It's like I'm one of Dad's girlfriends," she finally admitted to herself. As soon as she saw the root of her pound/pain link, we were able to work through and release it. Elaine understood why she felt undeserving of a thin, normal-weight body. She understood why she feared male attention, and why she felt guilty about being attractive. She had also changed her mental image of her weight, so now she could picture "150" on her bathroom scale.

Within two months, the 150-pound goal was a reality. Elaine no longer feared regaining the weight, and she'd learned to be assertive when dealing with the attention directed her way by men. Inappropriate advances, in the form of sexual harassment, were dealt with through normal company channels. More harmless types of male attention she simply shrugged off as a normal part of female life. Elaine learned that "nice" girls do get whistled at. And sometimes they even enjoy it.

What Is Your Self-Image?

There's an old saying that I believe bears a lot of truth: "God wouldn't give us the ability to dream, without also giving us the ability to make the dream come true." I think most of us know, deep inside, what our God-given dream is and who our real "me" is in all respects: looks, lifestyle, occupation, and personality.

But what would your "fantasy you" be like? That is, if you could change yourself and become any "you" that you desired, what would you be like? What would you look like? How would you act? What kind of job would you aspire to? What kind of home life would you have?

This fantasy is your "blueprint" to your God-given dream life. You can choose to completely remodel your present life situation, or just do a little rearranging. I used my blueprint to make some major overhauls, and that enterprise on my part literally saved my life.

When you are not fulfilling your mission or purpose, you experience pressure and discomfort. Something just feels wrong. For me, I had this sense of time urgency—the fear that I'd die before I accomplished what I was destined to do. Believe me, this emotional distress caused me a lot of stomachaches; the pressure of not following my blueprint was eating away at me!

When I got on the right track and started following my mental plan—to be a psychologist and a bestselling author, to have an attractive figure and a great relationship and to live on the water, it seemed like I was preparing to climb Mount Kilimanjaro for the first time. I wasn't sure I was going to get to the top, but I sure needed to try!

Something that really helped me achieve my goals, besides my daily affirmations and visualizations, was writing down all my wishes. One of my professors, a woman whom I admired, gave my class an assignment to write down every one of our wildest dreams. I wrote everything I could think of, like a kid with a Sears Christmas wishbook catalog. Then I put the list away and didn't think about it further.

About three years later, I found the list among some papers, and guess what? I had accomplished everything I had written down, from an exotic vacation, to the type of car I owned, to graduating, to being a published author, to much closer relationships with my two sons. Everything in my life reflected what I had written on that "wish" list.

Research on the writing-out of goals has confirmed the power and effectiveness of this practice. There's something about the physical act of writing, combined with seeing those words on paper, that activates more brain cells than does ordinary thinking. The goals become inscribed in your brain, and your actions reflect your expectation that, "I will achieve my goals."

I know that making changes in your life is difficult, painful even. I traveled a long, hard journey myself, and many times I felt discouraged and considered giving up. But always, this pressure deep inside of me kept pushing me, pushing me. That pressure was God, urging me to fulfill His mission, purpose, and plan—something that He wants all of us to do.

As your pressure is eased—because you are following your true path—your appetite for food will naturally lessen. As you lose weight, you will find that this change in your body and figure will inspire new experiences, some of them stressful, but many of them pleasant.

It's very likely that as you lose your pounds of pain, your relationships will evolve and grow, too. You will be like a room that has been closed for years and is suddenly opened to the sunlight and fresh air. The light will reveal some dusting, cleaning, and repairs that are needed, but the light will also attract many beautiful sights, experiences, and beings. You might also find that the light will repel some people in your life who desperately cling to negative beliefs. You may find that you need to say good-bye to these people who insist on staying in the "dark," as they will only bring you down.

As you stop overeating, you may also become painfully aware of life situations that trouble you. Food, for so many, is used as a means of blocking out conscious awareness of troubling marriages, unfulfilling jobs, financial difficulties, and family strife. When you remove the excess food from your life, you become more aware of EVERY-THING around you, both the good and the bad. Naturally, there will be times when you will be tempted to dive right back into overeating, but the best way to avoid reverting to old ways is to be truthful with yourself about your motives.

As you begin to realize you are overeating, ask yourself the important question, "WHY am I eating this?" As I've mentioned several times before, the sheer act of questioning yourself will help jolt you back into awareness. You automatically gain more control over your actions when you are truthful with yourself about your motives and intentions.

Remember: every time you put food in your mouth, you are deciding what size body you will have. When you choose to eat a lot of food, especially high-fat food, you are choosing a high-fat figure. The day you stop blaming your spouse, your children, your schedule, your job, your finances, your genetics, your thyroid, your metabolism, or your age for your weight—is the day you'll begin choosing to lose the weight and keep it off.

I understand how tempting it is to use external circumstances as a reason to stay fat. I had the perfect "excuse" to remain overweight:

I had borne two children and had come from a long line of overweight women. However, I chose not to accept these excuses as my reality. And I'm happy that, in recent years, my mother and my maternal grandmother have also decided to adopt fat-free lifestyles. We rejected blame and accepted responsibility for choosing our body sizes!

The vexing dilemma behind this wonderful choice is the knowledge that you—and only you—are in the driver's seat when it comes to the number of pounds you carry on your body. But here's a question for you: Is the fact that you are completely responsible for your weight a burdensome responsibility or a joyful choice? The former is a heavy, ponderous thought, while the latter is a light, carefree idea. And since our thoughts reflect our body weight, it's best to look at the situation as an *opportunity*.

You are free to choose!

CAN THERAPY HELP ME?

"Of all the destructive words in common use, surely one of the most powerful is the word 'impossible.' More people may have failed by using that one word than almost any other in the English language."

—Norman Vincent Peale

I BELIEVE THAT all abuse survivors, especially sexual abuse survivors, can benefit from *appropriate psychotherapy.* If you are thinking about going to a therapist, here are the benefits that you can expect to reap:

- Feeling more accepting of yourself

- Liking yourself a lot more

- Sleeping more soundly at night, with fewer nightmares and/or bouts of insomnia

- Less compulsion to overeat, overdrink, or use drugs

- Fewer relationship difficulties, such as arguments, irritability

- Better skills with respect to selecting romantic partners

- More ability to concentrate and focus

- Increased motivation to take good care of yourself

- Feeling more organized

- Feeling more relaxed about yourself and about life in general

- Better relationships with your children

- Better understanding or memory of your childhood

- Being more attuned to the feelings of friends and relatives

These are just some of the benefits of *appropriate psychotherapy*, which is a key term encompassing three essential elements:

1. The therapist must be experienced in treating sexual abuse survivors. More and more psychotherapists are specializing in this area because there is so much knowledge and information to absorb in order to effectively treat abused clients.

You can identify a trained sexual abuse therapist in a number of different ways. If you belong to a support group, other members can make recommendations. In addition, *Yellow Page* advertisements for psychologists often mention key phrases such as "Women's Issues," "Abuse Survivors," or "Adult Children of Alcoholics" (even if your parent wasn't an alcoholic, therapists in that field have experience in dealing with abuse issues).

Be sure to choose a licensed psychotherapist with at least a master's degree in psychology or social work. This graduate education provides vital training for therapists and helps them gain the maturity and skills not afforded at the undergraduate level.

Important: Never allow an unqualified person who calls her- or himself a "counselor" (a title used by many of the popular weight-loss programs) to delve deeply into your psychological issues. These untrained persons—who may very well be concerned people with good intentions—can do a lot more harm than good. They simply don't have the skills, training, or experience to separate their own issues from their clients'.

2. When meeting with a therapist for the first time (let's assume she's female for these purposes), make sure you feel comfortable

enough to be completely open with her. Ask yourself during the first session: Do I like this therapist on a personal level? Do I feel I can open up to her? Are her words nonjudgmental? Will she expect me to take her advice and direction, or will she allow me to make my own choices and decisions?

Don't worry about offending the therapist if you choose not to return for subsequent sessions. Therapists know they can't be everything to everybody and that some clients won't connect well with them. Therapy professionals don't take it personally when a client "shops around" and then decides to be treated by a different person. Besides, if the therapist does take it personally, this would not be the type of person you would want to be "helped" by in the first place!

3. The third element integral to *appropriate psychotherapy* is understanding that when it comes to treating sexual abuse, there are three types of therapists:

a. The first type includes those who are inexperienced with sexual abuse, and either downplay the significance of this trauma, avoid delving into the issue with the client at all, or give unhealthful advice. Ask your potential therapist how many cases of sexual abuse she has dealt with, and then listen to how she answers that question.

b. The second type of therapist believes that all women with eating disorders have been sexually abused. Beware of these types of therapists! They probably employ a cookie-cutter, simplistic philosophy and try to make all their clients conform to the same diagnosis and treatment. They are also the therapists responsible for creating the current "false memory" hysteria—they actually encourage clients to say they suddenly remember being molested by their parents. This situation creates massive disruptions within families—sometimes on a permanent basis. You can spot a "cookie-cutter" therapist pretty easily. She will *tell you*—as if it's an indisputable fact—that you've been sexually abused even if you've never brought up the subject. If this happens, find another therapist immediately.

c. The third type of therapist is experienced and openminded, someone who will really listen to you. She will help you deal with emotional pain connected to memories of abuse if you happen to actually remember sexual abuse incidents during the course of therapy. However, she won't tell you what has happened to you; she will emotionally support you while you tell her—and yourself—what occurred in the past. This is the best therapist for you. Don't quit until you find her.

Many female sexual abuse survivors choose same-sex therapists because they feel awkward discussing embarrassing details about the abuse with male therapists. I have met and worked with many highly qualified male therapists who work very effectively with sexual abuse survivors. However, these men are aware that female abuse survivors might shun them, and they are not offended by being passed over for a woman.

In the two all-women psychiatric hospitals where I was an administrator, 95 percent of the staffs were composed of women. The few men on staff tried their best to help their patients regain some trust in men, but there were still some unavoidable problems, such as the time a male nurse was in the unisex rest room, standing and urinating like a normal man. One of the female patients accidentally opened the door to the single-stall restroom and saw the male nurse's penis. She practically collapsed out of surprise and embarrassment, and the incident triggered a lot of issues surrounding her original sexual abuse episodes.

As far as financial issues are concerned, most health insurance policies cover part of the outpatient therapy cost for psychotherapy. Also, the majority of therapists will work with you to create a fee schedule that fits your budget. These therapists are aware that if therapy costs so much that it creates money problems, you won't feel any better about your life. They want you to come in for treatment, and they'll slash the price of therapy sessions to help you. My personal policy has always been to offer therapy at absolutely no cost to two patients per case load. It's my way of giving back, to help people who otherwise couldn't afford therapy. And believe me, they receive the same quality of therapy as someone paying full price.

156 ❧

What about outpatient therapy versus checking into a psychiatric hospital for a couple of weeks? Well, most insurance companies insist that before they'll cover the cost of inpatient psychiatric care, you first try outpatient therapy. I agree. I believe that with any type of health care—whether for physical or emotional ailments, it's best to try the least intrusive method first.

Usually, people who require inpatient care are:

- suicidal, and in need of 24-hour supervision just to stay alive;

- delusional, hallucinating, or dissociating; or

- those whose home and/or work life is keeping them continually sick, and who literally need to remove themselves from an unhealthy environment in order to get better.

There are advantages to receiving inpatient care over outpatient therapy, especially for sexual abuse survivors who compulsively overeat. Let's say, for example, that you're trying to work through intense memories of sexual abuse by seeing your therapist on your lunch hour. You're going to hold back a lot of your emotions just to maintain your composure so you can return to work without mascara running down your cheekbones from crying so much. In a psychiatric hospital, you don't have to worry about your job or your makeup. You can dive right into your emotions and stay with them until the issues are resolved.

Another benefit to inpatient care is that psychiatric hospitals attuned to abuse and overeating issues will monitor your eating. While this may trigger rebellion in patients with control issues connected to eating, it will also serve a positive purpose. If that food has been keeping a lid on your memories and emotions, your feelings will be closer to the surface if you're not compulsively overeating. So, the hospital environment that monitors your eating may help you to access your important thoughts and feelings about the abuse.

You can also give yourself this intense type of treatment on an outpatient basis by combining psychotherapy with attendance at Overeaters Anonymous (O.A.) meetings, where you will be assigned a sponsor. This type of combination therapy will help you access many abuse-related memories and thoughts.

The O.A. meetings and sponsor will help you monitor your eating and abstain from any "binge foods" (usually those with refined white flour or processed sugar). By regulating your eating, you'll be more apt to focus on profound abuse issues while seeing your psychotherapist.

It's important to attend O.A. meetings that are compatible with your personality and lifestyle. I recommend attending three different O.A. meetings before choosing one that you'll attend regularly. Look for a meeting with signs that group members are healthy, and not just sitting around making excuses or feeling sorry for themselves. A good way to assess the situation is to discern if at least three or four group members have abstained from compulsive overeating for over one year (long-term abstainers announce their success at the beginning of meetings).

At the end of the meeting, sponsors will raise their hands. A sponsor is someone whom you will talk to on the phone, or in person, every day. You will tell that person what you plan to eat, as a way of nailing down an eating plan, as opposed to impulsively deciding to overeat. It is frightening in the beginning to approach a sponsor, and many people feel intimidated by the process. Also, some people procrastinate before getting a sponsor, waiting for the "perfect person" to appear. The sponsor relationship really helps compulsive overeaters break out of compulsive overeating. So, take a deep breath and walk up to one of the sponsors, put out your hand, and just say, "I need a sponsor." The sponsor will do all the rest!

It's important to choose a sponsor who has abstained from compulsive overeating for at least one-and-a-half years, preferably longer. Always choose a same-sex sponsor and don't let anyone tell you otherwise. Male and female issues are just too different for an opposite-sex sponsor to maintain a productive long-term relationship with you.

Other Support Systems that Work

Not every person who undergoes therapy connected to weight loss requires intensive psychotherapy. Some people just need a little support while they change their eating and exercise habits. I've turned away several people from psychotherapy because there really were no clinical issues apparent. These women, who came to me for weight-loss support, were really better off at Weight Watchers—which is exactly where I sent them.

In the absence of a history of abuse, many people successfully lose weight—and keep it off—through the Weight Watchers program. The two things that make this program superior to the other diet organizations are: They don't pretend to be psychotherapists, and they offer balanced diets (although some are too high in sodium and artificial sweeteners for my taste).

But on the whole, I believe that Weight Watchers provides appropriate support. This group discusses lifestyle changes without delving into deep psychological issues. They don't use hard-sell or bait-and-switch advertising techniques. They offer group forums where people can share their hard-won successes and dieting challenges.

At the other extreme, I've done research on morbidly obese people who used bariatric surgery—"stomach stapling"—as a means of weight loss. This is definitely a radical approach to losing weight, one that carries the same health risks of any major surgery—including infection and death.

A California-based company called Comprehensive Weight Management asked me to write a psychological behavior-modification program for their patients who had had bariatric surgery. At first, I was very, very skeptical about this procedure, primarily because I knew of someone who died shortly after his stomach-stapling surgery ten years ago.

But my research revealed two things that surprised me: One is that the operation has changed radically in the last ten years, and is even touted by the National Institute of Health as a "viable option" for treating morbid (100 pounds or more overweight) obesity. In other words, the operation's safety record is very high now. Many doctors argue that when someone carries 100 extra pounds on the body, the risks of obesity outweigh the risks of the operation.

However, more important to me were the personal experiences that were recounted to me by the women who'd undergone the operation. These women were so happy to have had the opportunity to have this operation! Over and over again, I heard stories from women who had been so obese that they were practically bedridden. They couldn't work, play with their kids, or have sex with their husbands. In other words, they didn't have much of a life. And the prospect of trying out another traditional diet didn't appeal to them, as it could have taken them three years to drop all their excess weight.

The surgery was their way of making a forced choice. Following the surgery, these women had no alternative but to eat extremely small portions of food. Also, both before and after the surgery, these women underwent intensive psychotherapy, which allowed years of pent-up emotions and memories to flood to the surface. A staff psychologist and my behavior-modification program were available to guide and support them, as well.

Yes, my position on bariatric surgery certainly changed after spending time with these post-operative patients. Many times I heard these women say, "I would have died from the fat without this surgery. I needed to be forced to give up food so I could get in touch with the feelings that made me eat so much."

Indeed, anyone who becomes 100, 200, or more pounds overweight has few prospects for a normal life without radical intervention. I would hope, however, that bariatric surgery is viewed as a last-ditch attempt after every other method is tried and exhausted. No type of surgery ought to be viewed as a cure-all. After all, these stomach-stapling patients have to completely modify their old eating habits or risk rupturing their stapling lines. And the only way they can abstain from overeating is by turning to the intensive psychotherapy I've described.

Remember, there's nothing wrong with asking for help. If you're like most overeaters I've worked with, you are a very competent, bright person who usually has a lot of control over her life. It's frustrating to know that there is this one area of your life that is out of control—especially when you know what you can do to address it! That's why relying on different methods of support, such as a self-help book like this one, a therapist, or a support group, can give you that extra impetus we all need from time to time.

Keep going. You're doing a great job to have read this far, and there's so much more to learn. Don't forget: *You're worth all the effort!*

CHAPTER THIRTEEN

LISTENING TO FOOD CRAVINGS

"I was angry with my friend:
I told my wrath, my wrath did end.
I was angry with my foe:
I told it not, my wrath did grow."
—William Blake

IF YOU EAT one piece or serving of food—a candy bar, slice of cake, hamburger, or whatever—it doesn't necessarily mean you are trying to regulate your mood and energy levels. But if you feel compelled to consume large portions of a certain type of food *all of a sudden*, you are most likely eating to anesthetize troubling emotions. That is, you're experiencing tension, depression, anxiety, or boredom (which is really loneliness combined with the frustration that life is too routine), and you want to feel better fast.

The chemicals, ingredients, textures, tastes, and smells in most foods directly affect emotions and energy levels. After studying the individual effects of many of the mood/energy-regulating properties of certain foods, I've concluded that there is a very definite correlation between food cravings and emotional states.

Here's an example of the cyclical nature of this interrelationship: Betty feels depressed, so she reaches for a food that she knows intuitively from past experience will ease her depression—chocolate ice cream. It makes her feel better because of its natural antidepressant ingredients, texture, and, of course, taste. However, she consumes so much ice cream that she feels even more depressed later. This depression, stemming from her weight problem and other problematic issues in her life, compels her to eat even more chocolate ice cream the next day. And the cycle goes on and on, sometimes for a lifetime.

Without giving you a complex chemistry lecture, let me briefly explain how a food such as chocolate ice cream functions as an antidepressant. When you look at the combination of effects from the ingredients in this dessert, you will see that they trigger a reaction in people that is very similar to that resulting from the ingestion of prescription antidepressant drugs.

First, take a look at a breakdown of some of the properties in chocolate ice cream:

Ingredient/Characteristic	*Effect on Mood/Energy*
1. Choline	Soothing
2. L-Tryptophane mixed with carbohydrate	Calming
3. Phenylethylamine (P.E.A.— the so-called "love drug")	Feeling loved
4. Theobromine	Temporarily energizing
5. Tyramine	Temporarily energizing
6. Caffeine	Temporarily energizing
7. Magnesium	Relaxing
8. Pyrazine	Pleasure inducing
9. Fat	Calming and filling
10. Sugar	Temporarily energizing
11. Creamy texture	Comforting

And this is just a partial list! It does show, however, that chocolate ice cream both soothes and comforts you while, at the same time, re-energizing you temporarily. In other words, after eating chocolate ice cream, you feel renewed and ready to go—similar to the way you would feel if you were taking prescription antidepressant drugs. As far as I'm concerned, chocolate ice cream is an incredibly powerful "drug," and you can purchase it over the counter!

Chocolate frozen yogurt produces a similar effect, but because it may lack fat or sugar, yogurt won't sedate you as effectively as ice cream does. Also, carob, which is often used instead of chocolate in "health" foods, doesn't have the same chemical properties as chocolate, so carob yogurt or ice cream is in another category altogether.

Most of the other foods that people commonly overeat have similar food-mood correlations. Through my treatment of, and discussion with, clients all across the country, I have found that the connection between food, mood, and emotions depicted on the chart that follows almost always exists.

People in all walks of life have asked me what their food cravings say about their personality. I base my answer on the material that I've compiled in the following chart. And these people almost always exclaim in response, "You're absolutely right! That's exactly how I am."

I really went out on a limb when I appeared on talk shows hosted by Phil Donahue, Geraldo Rivera, and Sally Jessy Raphael, respectively. I asked the three hosts to tell me which foods they tend to binge on or have cravings for. Interestingly enough, they all mentioned that they tend to crave food that is salty and spicy. On national television, I unhesitatingly told each of them that people who crave or overeat salty, spicy foods usually also crave stimulation and excitement. All three talk-show hosts confirmed that what I said was true.

People who eat these types of foods tend to take huge risks in life. They face challenges head-on, and if they fail, they try again. This is certainly true for Donahue, Geraldo, and Sally Jessy. Without these qualities, they probably wouldn't be able to withstand the pressure of being in the national spotlight and dealing with ratings wars.

What follows is a list of commonly overeaten foods, together with the emotions that usually precipitate a craving for them. Each item on this list contains chemicals, textures, tastes, and smells that break down in much the same manner as chocolate ice cream did.

The only exception to the information provided on this chart is if an extremely positive or negative emotion is associated with a certain food. For example, if Grandma always served you chicken soup when you were sick, you may feel nauseated every time you smell chicken broth—regardless of the chemical properties in the soup. Or, if Mom always fixed you cookies and milk after school, you may associate that snack with feelings of love and warmth.

In general, though, I've found my research findings on food and mood, as outlined below, to be incredibly accurate. This chart will not only help you understand what is behind your food cravings, but will also give you the wherewithal to address these underlying emotions instead of covering them up with food.

Food	*Associated Emotional/Personality Traits*
1. Chocolate candy bars, plain	You desire stimulation, or feel deprived of love.
2. Crunchy chocolate candy, chocolate bars with nuts	You feel frustrated, anxious, or angry due to tension or lack of love.
3. Chocolate ice cream	You feel depressed, usually because of tension or difficulty in a relationship.
4. Chocolate chip, rocky road, or any crunchy chocolate ice cream	You are holding in anger, or feel angry at yourself, resulting in depression.
5. Mint chocolate chip ice cream	You feel lethargic and frustrated because you have more responsibilities than you have time or motivation.
6. Chocolate pudding	You desire comfort, nurturing, and hugs.
7. Chocolate cake	You feel empty, insecure, possibly due to lack of love.

8. Hot chocolate

You have built up hurt feelings throughout the day, and now you want to soothe your ego so you can sleep.

9. Crunchy, high-fat foods

You feel empty because of frustration or anger.

10. Spicy foods topped with dairy products (pizza with extra cheese; Mexican food with cheese and sour cream)

You feel depressed because life seems dull.

11. Dairy products (cheese, yogurt, etc.)

You feel depressed or unloved; you desire nurturing and comfort.

12. Baked goods, pastries

You feel tense and need to relax. You may also feel that your life is empty.

13. Crunchy foods topped with dairy products (crackers and cheese; chips and dip; nachos with cheese and no salsa; salad with blue cheese dressing, etc.)

You are holding in anger, resentment, and/or frustration, resulting in depression.

14. Sugary sweets

You want to feel energetic, or to overcome burnout.

15. Colas (diet or regular)

You feel overwhelmed by work or chores; you want to have more energy (including sexual energy).

16. Hamburgers and other high-fat fast foods

You feel empty or dissatisfied with some aspects of life. You may also feel insecure or inadequate in some area of life.

By understanding the food-mood connections, you'll be in a better position to control your compulsive binge eating. The best method to use in this regard may almost sound too easy to you. However, the feedback that I receive from my thousands of clients and workshop attendees is that IT WORKS.

Here it is: The next time you suddenly feel very hungry—meaning, out-of-the-blue hungry—promise me that you won't go near any food for 15 minutes. Get out of the house if you have to. If you're at work, go into the ladies' room or some other nonfood area. Throw any tempting food items down the garbage disposal if you can't leave the area you're in for some reason. But don't put the food in the trash, because sometimes desperate people dig it back out again. Bottom line: No matter what you have to do, don't eat anything for 15 minutes after first feeling hunger pangs.

Then, ask yourself: "Could I possibly be feeling an emotion I'm uncomfortable with? Am I feeling drained or tense? Am I trying to use food as a pick-me-up?" Most people find that by using this two-step method, they're able to control their food cravings to a greater extent, thus exercising more control over their appetite and actions.

Physically Based Cravings

Not all food cravings are triggered by emotions, though. There are very real physical reasons why you crave certain foods, usually due to vitamin or mineral deficiencies.

When the body lacks certain essential minerals, vitamins, and amino acids, food cravings function like a signal, similar to a low-fuel light on a car dashboard. There are often deficiencies with respect to minerals such as magnesium, chromium, calcium, the B vitamins, vitamin C, and amino acids such as tryptophan.

Tryptophan—commonly found in proteins such as dairy and meat products—is a catalyst for creating the brain chemical serotonin. As mentioned in chapter 10, serotonin plays a major role in determining your mood, energy level, and the quality of your sleep. When serotonin becomes depleted, the body signals include carbohydrate cravings, mood swings, irritability, fatigue, a decreased desire for sex, and insomnia.

Magnesium, chromium, and calcium are also crucial to your physical and mental health. When your body is low on any of these minerals, your energy level drops. You may feel somewhat depressed without really knowing why. You want to eat, not only to replenish these minerals, but also due to your desire to draw energy from the natural stimulants in food.

B vitamins also play an important role in energy regulation. Unfortunately, whenever we eat "junk food" or anything that contains "empty" calories, we deplete our body's B vitamins because it takes B vitamins to digest any substance we ingest. If we eat potato chips, for example, we'll use B vitamins to digest them. Since the potato chips don't contain any B vitamins, we will have used B vitamins without replacing them. We'll be in a B-vitamin deficit, and this will trigger food cravings.

When C vitamins are at a low level in the body, we may crave salad, tomatoes, or other fruits and vegetables. Unfortunately, many compulsive overeaters turn to high-fat versions of salads and vegetable dishes to fulfill these otherwise-healthful cravings.

Vitamin, mineral, and amino acid depletions occur because of tension, environmental or dietary pollutants, too-stringent dieting, alcohol or drug abuse (including caffeine abuse), insomnia, or the onset of the menstrual cycle. The eating plan in this book circumvents food cravings by providing a menu high in vitamins, minerals, and amino acids.

I think it's important to eat a very healthy diet in order to feel and look your best. What's the point of *looking* slim and trim if you can't enjoy it because you don't *feel* good? I'm also a great believer in taking vitamin and mineral supplements. Vitamins B-6 and B-12, and the minerals magnesium, chromium picolinate, and calcium, all help combat food cravings. If your body has adequate amounts of these substances, you'll be less apt to overeat.

EATING IN SECRET,
EATING IN SHAME

"He that respects himself is safe from others; He wears a coat of mail that none can pierce."
—Henry Wadsworth Longfellow

EVERY EVENING after dinner, Brenda patiently waited until her family went to bed. She always managed to come up with a good excuse for why she wanted to stay up. "I want to finish this chapter in the book I'm reading," she'd tell her husband, or "That comedian I like is on TV tonight."

She wouldn't dare admit her true motivation for staying awake while the others slept—to be alone with her favorite dessert of ice cream and cake. About a half hour after her husband retired for the night and Brenda was certain that she couldn't hear him rustling around in the bedroom anymore, she'd make her move.

Quietly, in fact so softly that no one could possibly hear her, Brenda would slip into the kitchen. And then, as carefully as she could, Brenda would open the freezer door and pull out a carton of ice cream. She'd hold her breath while lifting the carton's lid so the sound of the air suction and cardboard rubbing against one another wouldn't awaken anyone.

Sometimes, Brenda would think she heard someone coming, so she'd quickly shove the ice cream carton into a cupboard. But when she was alone and had successfully retrieved her ice cream and cake without a sound, Brenda would stand in the laundry room where no one could see her.

Being alone with her desserts was sheer bliss to Brenda. She was by herself, where no one could criticize her for going off her diet or cause her to really stop and think about what she was doing.

In truth, though, Brenda wasn't alone in her behavior. There are thousands, perhaps millions, of "Closet Bingers"—people who feel the need to sneak and hide when eating their favorite food. Some conceal candy bars in the bottom of their purse; some keep cupcakes hidden in the glove compartment; some stoop down behind open refrigerator doors so that others won't see them eating with utter abandonment. And I've had clients tell me that they kept food hidden in the bathroom, where they could eat in complete privacy.

But the person the closet binger most wants to hide from is *herself.*

Closet Binging and Self-Esteem

I've talked to and treated hundreds of Closet Bingers who were single and living alone. And yet, even though they weren't sharing their living space with anyone, they were still afraid that someone else might "catch" them eating something fattening.

My client, Sue, comes to mind when I think of someone who would sneak-eat, even though there was no one in her life to hide the eating from. During her first therapy session, Sue blurted out that the only way she was going to be able to recover from compulsive overeating was to remove her large stash of candy bars from her car. I walked out to the parking lot to help her, and together we filled up my medium-sized office trash can with boxes of Hershey's bars, Nestlé Crunch bars, and dozens of crumpled old candy wrappers.

With Closet Bingers such as Sue, the compulsive nature of eating isn't just wrapped up in the appeal of the food. Instead, the "rush" involved in sneaking is a large part of the appeal. Most people have enjoyed the thrill of doing something somewhat naughty. And even though there is that heart-pounding fear involved in being caught, there is also a form of excitement inherent in such an act. So, the Closet Binger who successfully completes an eating binge may actually congratulate herself for getting away with an ingeniously master-minded plan.

Closet Binging is also a silent form of rebellion against real or perceived pressures to be a "good girl," pressures that usually stem from childhood experience.

For example, Sue learned early on in life that attention and praise were heaped upon her when she acted "sweet" and when she got *A*'s on her report card. Her parents constantly referred to her as "our problem-free child." So how could Sue ever let her parents down? She couldn't. Sue found that complying with others' wishes was the fastest route to gaining approval—a habit that she carried into adulthood.

However, it's normal for overly compliant people to rebel from time to time. No one can maintain a false persona of being in a cheerful, understanding mood on a continuous basis. In my practice, I've found that many "good girls" silently try to regain control over their lives by gorging on food when others aren't looking.

Many times, these women grew up in households where a lot of attention was paid to their physical appearance and weight. Messages such as, "Better cut down on the calories because your rear end is starting to get big," are common in Closet Binger households. In other words, part of being a "good girl" implicitly means watching out for fattening foods and calories. Sadly, the young Closet Binger is usually unaware of the fact that it is *her* body, and therefore her right to regulate what foods she eats and what figure she chooses to maintain.

Sneak-eating usually starts in childhood. This is not a simple case of children stealing cookies from the cookie jar, although that *can* be one symptom of early childhood Closet Binging. Instead, sneak-eating is a process whereby the person feels unsafe indulging in pleasurable obsessive eating around others. There's an underlying fear that if she is caught eating something "bad" (ice cream, cake, candy, etc.), that the "privilege" of eating this food will be suspended. And, on top of that, her additional punishment will be that the other person will view her in a less-than-perfect light.

To the Closet Binger, it's easier to hide imperfect behavior such as obsessive eating from the rest of the world, and to present the face of a competent superwoman or supergirl for everyone else to see. But she also denies to herself that she's sneak-eating. In other words, she's not only hiding from others but from herself, too.

What's particularly interesting to me is that sneak-eaters are often extremely accomplished women. Every aspect of their life—career, academics, material possessions, and family life—appears to be under control. But, for the sneak-eater, a very crucial part of life—revolving around eating and weight gain—is completely out of control.

Breaking the Eat-and-Sneak Cycle

Closet Bingers who examine their motivations for sneak-eating are far less inclined to persist in this practice than people who never take a look at their reasons for doing it.

My client, Samantha, for example, said that I was the first person she'd ever admitted her sneak-eating habits to. As a result of this discussion, Samantha found that she wasn't comfortable the next time she began to sneak-eat. After being honest with me, it was difficult to hide what she was really doing from herself.

I believe that being honest with oneself is a key factor in breaking any addictive cycle because so much of compulsive eating, drinking, shopping, and so on, is really just a way to avoid looking inside oneself. In other words, many people engage in addictions because they're running away from something deep within themselves or their lives that they don't want to scrutinize.

Many of my Closet Binger clients were sneak-eating to avoid honestly looking at their unhappy marriages or jobs. Other clients were afraid to acknowledge all of the anger they were harboring within. And still others were struggling with insecurities—"Am I inadequate?"—and mistakenly thought that if they admitted this fear to themselves, it would undoubtedly become a reality.

Abuse survivors, guarded and untrusting of others, often sneak-eat because it doesn't feel safe to indulge in the very private affair called eating, out in the open. Others sneak-eat to avoid ridicule or scorn.

Eating in private isn't unhealthful in and of itself. The problem is that the act of sneak-eating fuels massive and obsessive consumption of food. When you fear being caught, or you feel you're doing something wrong or "naughty," your anxiety level is elevated. The anxiety then triggers an eating binge. So, for all intents and purposes, you overeat to quell the nervousness triggered by overeating in the first place! Ironic, isn't it? Yet, there *are* steps that Closet Bingers can take when the sneak-eating urge crops up:

1. Remember that no matter whom you hide from, or how much you deny to yourself what you're doing, the calories from your binge will manifest themselves as fat on *your* body. In the end, it probably doesn't matter to anyone else, as much as it does to you, how much you weigh or how you feel inside your body.

2. Also consider this: Sneak-eating really isn't as much fun as you may believe. If you're really honest with yourself, I think you'll agree that sneak-eating feels crummy and makes you feel bad about yourself.

3. Start keeping a food diary, and write down every single thing you eat and drink. The diary doesn't have to be anything fancy; most of my clients just buy a little 3 x 5-inch notepad at the grocery store and use one page per day. Just be sure to keep it handy so you won't forget to write in it. Even if you're ashamed of something you ate, write it down anyway. This will not only get you in the habit of honestly coming to terms with what you're putting in your body, it will also remind you to keep your portions small and your fat content low.

Once you honestly confront the Closet Binging issue, it becomes much easier to eradicate it from your life. I've seen many people achieve great success by employing the methods described in this chapter. And the good news is that after putting this habit behind them, it is usually gone for good!

LIQUIDS: THIRST, WATER,
AND ALCOHOL

"It is necessary to the happiness of a man that he be mentally faithful to himself."
—Thomas Paine

THE LIQUIDS you drink can be just as important to your diet as the foods you eat when you're trying to maintain your weight. Many dieters—particularly "chocoholics" who tend to abuse psychoactive (mood-altering) chemicals in ordinary foods—drink too much diet cola.

The reason I say "too much" is because diet or regular cola, if consumed in too great a quantity, makes dieting a difficult process and even slows weight loss. There are three problems associated with drinking diet colas while trying to lose weight:

1. A 12-ounce can of diet cola contains roughly 70 milligrams of sodium. This may not seem high when you consider that the recommended daily sodium consumption for a dieting woman is 1,000 milligrams. However, consider this: If you drink four sodas a day, that's 280 milligrams of sodium! And when you add that sodium to all the salt you normally consume in food, you can easily exceed the 1,000-milligram-per-day level.

Besides being linked to high blood pressure, the primary concern dieters have regarding sodium for dieters is that it causes water retention. Dieters struggling with weight plateaus often have to cut their diet cola consumption down to a maximum of two cans a day before weight loss can continue.

2. Colas contain about as much caffeine as a half cup of coffee. The caffeine in colas is made from kola nut extract, and regulations keep the caffeine content at a maximum of 0.02 percent of the soda.

However, when dieters drink a great deal of soda (over two cans a day), the caffeine amount accumulates; and nervous, excited, jittery, or anxious feelings may result. Also, one of the amino acids in the sweetener aspartame (NutraSweet brand sweetener) called "phenyla-lanine" acts as a natural stimulant, which makes some individuals feel dizzy, light-headed, or anxious. The resulting tension from caffeine and phenylalanine can trigger a desire to overeat, as the dieter seeks to calm down through the use of food.

3. Cola can reduce your magnesium levels, thereby triggering food cravings. A study conducted at East Tennessee State University found that phosphoric acid in cola binds with magnesium in the body, and extracts the latter. Each 12-ounce can of cola contains 36 milligrams of phosphoric acid, and the result is that 36 milligrams of magnesium are removed from the body.

In light of the information above, you can probably see why it's important to cut down or eliminate your consumption of soda. However, if you feel you can't live without diet cola, then limit your intake to two cans or 24 ounces a day.

A Half-Gallon a Day . . .

The ideal drink for dieters, as you may already know, is water. I recommend drinking at least one-half gallon a day. This may sound like an awful lot of liquid to consume, but what really works for me, as well as for my clients, is to get in the habit of keeping one-gallon bottles of purified water nearby at all times to help get you in the habit of drinking throughout the day. Buy several bottles at the store (they're not that expensive, especially compared to the price of cola), and carry one to work with you each day.

Water is beneficial to dieters for several reasons:

- It makes you feel full, so you won't be as hungry.
- It is actually more energizing than a cup of coffee, so you won't be as apt to reach for a sugary food to try and pep yourself up.
- It flushes salt out of the body, thereby reducing water retention.
- It also flushes out the residuals of burned body fat, a form of ash that remains in the body unless it is washed out with water.

I've found that the feeling of being deprived because you're drinking "plain old boring water" is negated by turning the water into a special drink. Two easy ways to accomplish this are to pour the water into a special, pretty glass and to garnish it with a slice of lemon or lime.

A Word about Alcohol

Perhaps the most striking observation I've made in working with compulsive overeaters is the high incidence (over 95 percent) of alcoholism in their extended family. Almost all of my clients had either parents or grandparents who drank alcohol in a dependent or abusive manner. Even my clients who initially denied that alcoholism ran in their family usually found, after asking other family members, that yes, Grandpa was, in fact, an alcoholic. Of course, nobody in the family ever talked about it. Instead, they'd say that Grandpa died of cirrhosis of the liver, a heart attack, or some other alcoholism-related disease.

The purpose of this discussion is not to point the finger of blame, as in "It's grandpa's fault" that you compulsively overeat. But it is important to understand the role that alcoholism may have played, or is playing, in your life.

The majority of studies on alcoholism in families overwhelmingly point to a genetic link that causes an alcoholic predisposition—that is, *there is a greater propensity toward alcoholism than in people from nonalcoholic families.* Although only about 10 percent of people in the general population develop problems with alcoholism, having one alcoholic parent in your family increases your chances of developing alcoholism more than 30 percent. And if your mother and your father were both alcoholic, your own risk is greater than 50 percent!

Sugar Addiction and Alcoholism

Alcohol and sugar are almost identical as far as their molecular structure is concerned. The result is that people prone to alcoholism have a reaction to sugar that mimics the alcoholic reaction to alcohol. This reaction manifests itself as a combination of changes in the brain's chemistry and electrical activity and a craving for more alcohol or sugar.

The alcoholic body has a difficult time distinguishing between alcohol and sugar and feels the need to binge on one or both substances, which makes sense when you consider that alcohol is created out of food: Wine is fermented fruit; beer is made from grain; vodka from potatoes, and so on.

I've also found that female children and grandchildren of alcoholics are more apt to choose refined sugar over alcohol as their "feel-good drug" of choice. I believe this occurs for two reasons:

1. Social pressures train young females to be "good little girls," motivating females to pick "the good girl's drug": sugar.

2. Most likely, the girl's mother was herself a compulsive eater and sugar binger. The little girl watched her mother overeat and use sugar as a tension-management tool, and this increased the likelihood that the girl would abuse sugar later on in life.

Those Abused by Alcohol Often Grow Up to Do the Same

Psychotherapists such as myself, who specialize in treating addictions, bear witness to a common family scenario: Compulsive overeaters and alcoholics are often married to each other. In many of my clients' families, we chart "family trees" of addictions running through the generations. The most prevalent pattern I've seen is that males abuse alcohol; and their wives, sisters, and daughters have eating disorders.

As stated above, part of this phenomenon stems from the pressure put on females to be "good girls." Women are more apt to choose a socially sanctioned substance—that is, food—to make themselves feel better. Men are more easily "forgiven," if you will, for sitting around with the guys and throwing down a few drinks.

The result is that women who do abuse alcohol often do so in private. As is the case with Closet Bingers who sneak-eat when no one is looking, Closet Drinkers gulp their wine, beer, and vodka in private. They don't want anyone to know they are drinking, and out of shame, they abuse alcohol when they are alone.

Those suffering from the pound/pain link are especially prone to alcohol abuse. Sexual, physical, and emotional abuse survivors often come from alcoholic households. Fathers who molest their daughters are usually drunk at the time, and the mother may be passed out on the sofa from an afternoon of drinking Screwdrivers. The little girl grows up watching her parents turn to alcohol to alleviate or manage tension. As an abuse survivor, she grows up feeling tense herself—since she hasn't learned how to relax and trust people—and so turns to alcohol, just as her parents "taught" her.

Researchers Singer and Petchers (1989) studied 48 adolescents who had been sexually abused and concluded that they were much more likely to abuse alcohol and other drugs than adolescents who had not been sexually abused. Other studies (Benward, 1975; Cohen, 1982; Rohsenow, 1988) have found that between 30 and 44 percent of people diagnosed as being addicted to drugs or alcohol have a history of sexual abuse. This is a much higher percentage than is found in the general population of nonsubstance abusers.

Studies of brain chemistry in alcoholics also point to physiological causes for alcoholism. We know that there are genetic predispositions toward alcoholism; in other words, you can inherit the desire to abuse alcohol. Several researchers have discovered that the brain chemical, serotonin, may be depleted in alcoholic brains. As you may recall from previous chapters, when serotonin is low, you feel lethargic or irritable. Researchers believe alcoholics may be self-medicating, attempting to compensate for the depleted serotonin by getting drunk.

Unfortunately, alcohol abuse results in further serotonin depletion. Serotonin is a chemical that forms in the brain as you sleep. Your brain doesn't store the substance; it must be created from scratch every night. What happens is this: Your body converts a body substance, melatonin, into the brain chemical, serotonin, during the Rapid Eye Movement (REM) phase of the nightly sleep cycle. If your REM sleep cycle is interrupted, you won't create enough serotonin. And then you'll wake up feeling groggy.

Excessive consumption of alcohol and other drugs interferes with REM sleep. If you drink too much before bed, you won't get enough REM sleep, and you'll wake up with a hangover from depleted serotonin. Those suffering from the pound/pain link may notice that they crave carbohydrates (breads, sweets, and starchy foods) when their serotonin is low.

Even worse, alcohol interferes with weight-loss efforts.

First, alcohol is very fattening. Just look at how many calories are in a typical drink, keeping in mind that most people have more than one drink at a sitting:

Alcoholic Beverage	*Calories Consumed*
Beer, 12 oz.	150
Brandy, 1 oz.	75
Champagne, dry, 4 oz.	105
Champagne, sweet, 4 oz.	160
Daiquiri, 3½ oz.	125
Distilled liquors (Gin, Rum, Vodka, Whisky, 80 proof, 1½ oz.)	100
Martini, 3½ oz.	140
Tom Collins, 10 oz.	180
Wine (red) 3½ oz.	85
(white) 3½ oz.	80

Second, alcohol slows the body down. It is a depressant. But, whoops! It especially slows down metabolism, the rate at which your body burns calories. So, not only does alcohol ADD calories to your body, but it also makes you burn those calories at a slower rate.

Finally—and you're probably aware of this from personal experience—if you've been drinking or you're hung-over, you're less likely to exercise. Even though a workout would probably make you feel much better, when you're tired or irritated, you just want to relax. So, you burn even fewer calories because your energy level is low.

There's nothing wrong with drinking alcohol in moderation (as long as you don't drive after doing so). It's just important to drink wisely and choose low-calorie alcoholic drinks such as dry white wine mixed with sparkling soda. Of course, people with predispositions toward alcoholism, as well as those who are confirmed alcoholics, are well advised to abstain completely from alcohol.

The support group, Alcoholics Anonymous (who could assist you in getting a sponsor if you desire one), in conjunction with psychotherapeutic help, can be of enormous assistance to you if you have decided that you wish to give up alcohol.

DIETING WITHOUT
DEPRIVATION

*"The smallest seed of faith is better than the
largest fruit of happiness."*
—Henry David Thoreau

Why Are There Recipes in This Book?

LET ME ANSWER some questions you may have about the inclusion
of menus and recipes in this book. As you may know, traditional
eating-disorder books rarely offer recipes. The authors usually dis-
courage any concentration on eating or weight loss. Traditional diet
books, on the other hand, discuss food, recipes, and eating to a greater
degree than they do behavior modification or emotional support.

I think these two extremes fail to offer the person suffering from
a pound/pain link what she really needs. I know from my clinical experience that people seeking to shed their pain, and shed their pounds,
want and need emotional and physiological guidance. It's no coincidence that most of my clients are "dieting experts" by the time they
meet me. They've been on every diet known to (wo)man, and can
practically recite the calorie, carbohydrate, and fat content of any food
you could name. After all, they're consumed—or might I say "tor-
tured"?—with thoughts of food, eating, grocery shopping, cooking,
and weight.

As I've mentioned previously, most of my clients are very intelligent women, often very successful in business and family matters.
They are accustomed to being in control, and it frustrates the hell out

of them that they can't manage their appetite and weight—especially when they know exactly how to do so. Yes, of course, these women know which actions will lead to successful weight loss, they just can't seem to implement this behavior in their lives on a consistent basis.

So, my psychotherapy practice is dually focused. First, I delve into the pain issues triggering the excessive appetite for food—that is, I help my clients to understand the pain, and then release it. Utilizing that process, weight naturally begins to drop off because the appetite normalizes.

Second, I discuss healthful lifestyles. This area involves relearning how to eat tasty, balanced, light meals. It also includes the incorporation of other "feel-good" changes into one's life—things like paying attention to your current relationships at home and work, exercising, meditating, staying aware of alcohol consumption, and so on.

You see, I'm not asking you to focus on your eating and weight. But I'm not asking you to ignore these areas either. While I believe the true essence of our beings is spiritual, and not material, we *do* have bodies that encase our souls and psyches. We all walk around with the bodies we've been issued, and these bodies can have a negative or positive influence on our emotional states. If you treat this body gently and pamper it with rest, exercise, and nurturing foods, it will return the favor by helping you feel good for a lifetime.

You can use the emotional and psychological suggestions in this book in conjunction with any healthful balanced meal plan and still lose a lot of weight. The suggested meal plans included in this chapter are simply guidelines that will give you an inkling of what has worked for my clients. In my psychotherapy practice, I've seen women of all ages and social and cultural backgrounds struggle with the "What do I eat?" dilemma. It's a question that comes up at least three times a day, so the one-week menu that I provide you with later on may give you some practical answers if you are plagued by this question, as well.

Moderation Is the Key

When trying to lose excess pounds, do you ever find yourself doing the following: You've just about had it with being overweight, so you decide to shed the excess pounds in a hurry. Therefore, you fix "conventional" diet meals consisting of cold, dry salads and steamed white fish devoid of sauce.

But how long does this type of eating plan last? Don't you get fed up with the bland taste, lack of texture, and homogeneity of "diet foods"?

I used to vacillate, as well, between extremely low-calorie, low-fat meals and high-calorie, high-fat menus. One week, I'd be suffering through cottage cheese and steamed vegetables, the next week I'd be making up for it by eating extra-cheese pizza and barbecued chicken. No wonder I suffered from the yo-yo syndrome of watching my weight go up and down, up and down, all those years!

It took me a while to incorporate the principle of "moderation" into my life, and especially into my eating and cooking habits. The best weight-loss plan, as you've read countless times, is one that yields a steady, slow weight-loss rate. Yeah, yeah, yeah, you may say to yourself when reading this, I'll go on a moderate diet. But first I want to get these ten pounds off, and I want to get them off now!

So, what about a compromise of sorts? How about an eating plan that allows for steady weight loss and the maintenance of high energy, and that also offers you delicious, interesting meals? What's the catch, you ask? Well, there is one, actually: You must cook your own meals. While it is possible to eat at restaurants and order low-fat, healthful foods, there are many "traps," such as huge portions, hidden fatty ingredients, high sodium, and the temptation of the dessert cart being wheeled by. Sure, you can heat up those frozen low-calorie dinners, but I think the portions are ridiculously small and the taste—if you can call it that—leaves a lot to be desired. You may feel deprived if you base your diet plan on those frozen meals, and as a result, you may end up eating two or three dinners to compensate. Then you're right back where you started from!

I've been preparing low-calorie, low-fat versions of my favorite dishes for several years now and have had hundreds of recipes published in various publications. My goal with every menu I plan is the same: I want it all! I strive for a meal that's extremely flavorful, that doesn't take too long to prepare, that my family will love, that doesn't use expensive or exotic ingredients, that provides variety, and, of course, that is low in fat and calories. The recipes included later on in this chapter are some of my favorites, and I urge you to try them.

Grocery List for the Sample Menu

If you're like me, a busy professional without a lot of extra time for meal planning and preparation, let me share one very useful tip: On Sunday, plan your menu for the entire week, and then go shopping with that meal plan written on a piece of paper. It's so time-consuming to try and figure out, every day, "What do I make for dinner?" Then, you have to go grocery shopping every evening, and that really cuts into your busy day (especially if you show up at the supermarket at peak time—around 5:00 or 6:00 P.M.).

So, these days, I'm in the habit of planning my week's menu every Sunday. I choose Sunday because I'm one of those shoppers who uses store cents-off coupons, and they appear in my Sunday newspaper supplements. So, after I read the paper, I peruse the coupons for menu ideas. Then I pull out my recipe files and write out seven dinner plans, from which I can write down my grocery list. Then, it's off to the supermarket to shop for the week. I do have to return to the store once, or at the most twice, during the week for those items I may have forgotten or run out of (or if my menu calls for fresh fish or poultry later in the week), but generally, the major part of the shopping task is taken care of on Sundays.

What follows is a sample grocery shopping list, based on the suggested menus in this book. If you normally don't shop with a plan and a list, you may want to copy this one (or take the book to the store) and see how you like it. Most people find that when they get organized and take care of important things such as shopping, it makes them feel that they have accomplished something. In that respect, it is a way to take care of oneself.

The sample menu and grocery shopping list is geared toward a family of four. You can divide or multiply, of course, to arrive at a menu that suits a smaller or larger family. Many of the grocery items are staples that you may already have around the house. If you don't, you'll find that condiments and spices such as mustard, honey, capers, and basil are handy to have around—and they last practically forever!

Sample Grocery Shopping List (family of four)

Produce
2 lbs.mushrooms
3 medium brown onions
2 red bell peppers, small
½ lb. Chinese snow peas
2 bunches green onions or scallions
1 lb.broccoli florets
1 garlic bulb, or one jar crushed garlic
2 heads lettuce, any variety
1 lb. tomatoes
4 baking potatoes
1 lb. new potatoes (small red)
Lemon, 1 large, or 2 medium
Carrots, 3 medium
Apples, 4 large
Bananas, 2 lbs. ripe

Dairy Products
1 lb. light butter or margarine
1 gallon skim or 1% milk
1 8-oz. package or tub, nonfat cream cheese
1 16-oz. tub low-fat (not nonfat) sour cream
1 8-oz. tub or dry package, Parmesan cheese, nonfat or reduced-fat
Eggs, one dozen medium or large
1 package, 6–8 oz, feta cheese (traditional style, crumbled or block)

Canned/Dry Goods

1 package, 12–16 oz. fettuccine noodles
1 package, 12–16 oz. angel hair pasta or vermicelli (thin spaghetti) noodles
1 package, 12–16 oz. Chinese or Yaki-Sobi noodles
2 14.5-oz. cans, chicken broth, reduced sodium and clear
5 cans stewed tomatoes
1 six-oz. can crabmeat, white
16 oz. of fat-free cereal

Spices/Condiments

Salad dressing, fat-free or very low-fat
Oregano
Thyme
Basil
Dill
Marjoram
Ground pepper
Ground ginger
Reduced sodium soy sauce
All-purpose flour
Dijon mustard
Honey
Olive oil, extra virgin, extra light
Capers, one jar

Poultry/Fish

4 filets of sole, approximately 1½ lbs. total
8 chicken breasts, approximately 2 lbs. total without bone
Turkey breast, approximately 1¾ lbs. total without bone
Salmon filet(s), approximately ¾ lb. total
Shrimp, medium size, uncooked, approximately 1 lb. total

Supplies/Utensils

Aluminum foil, at least 25 feet
Wire whisk for cooking sauces

As you probably realize by now, permanent weight loss requires the adoption of a healthy lifestyle. That means a life-long commitment to exercise and sensible eating. Radical approaches to weight loss, such as liquid diets or extremely restricted eating plans, only result in temporary drops in weight.

What's made it much easier for me to permanently incorporate moderate eating into my life is my habit of eating highly spiced dishes. A typical dinner for me is one loaded with bulk, nutritional value, and most of all—taste. For years, I've experimented with low-fat, yet "spiced-up" variations, on my favorite Italian, Mexican, Japanese, and Southern dishes.

Italian cooking is ideal for healthful, light eating if you avoid the heavy creams and cheeses in the traditional dishes. Since most Italian cooking revolves around pasta as opposed to meat, these meals already consist of a good amount of low-fat bulk.

My personal motto regarding "light" foods is this: If it tastes good, I'll eat it. But nonfat or low-fat foods that taste funny or tasteless are not acceptable to me. I'd rather eat the "real thing" in moderation than eat a large portion of some awful-tasting light food. For example, *non-fat* versions of sour cream, margarine, and cottage taste terrible to me. They're just not worth eating, no matter how many calories and fat grams I save! I'd rather eat a much smaller portion of *low-fat* sour cream, margarine, or cottage cheese, because I find them so much more enjoyable!

On the other hand, the fat-free versions of cream cheese, yogurt, Parmesan cheese, and shredded cheddar cheese taste remarkably good. I'll eat these any day.

So, to reiterate, if our meals consist of food that is too-small in portion, or that tastes bad or bland, we'll feel deprived. And if we feel deprived, we won't stick with that eating plan for very long. It will simply turn out to be one more temporary diet, followed by the regaining of the weight and a still-slower metabolism.

Nutritionists and medical doctors have also made note of another new dieting phenomenon that someone cleverly dubbed "The Entenmann's Diet." Some people are binge-eating fat-free foods, thinking that they can eat as much as they want. Of course, just because something is fat-free doesn't make it calorie-free. Fat-free cookies, muffins, and cakes chalk in at 50 to 250 calories each! If you eat a whole box of these fat-free goodies, you're ingesting 1,500-plus calories at one sitting.

Better to eat light and right. If you eat a variety of tasty dinner meals that are low-fat, you'll naturally lose weight. You'll feel full and satisfied and will be less apt to binge on a late-evening snack.

So, try cooking your favorite meals with lighter cooking methods. The little things you do can pare a lot of fat and calories off the menu, without sacrificing flavor. Here are a few of my fat-fighting cooking techniques:

— Taking the skin off a pound of chicken means 225 fewer calories and 29 fewer grams of fat.

— A pound of *dark* chicken meat has 150 more calories and 23 more grams of fat than a pound of *light* chicken meat.

— Using the minimum amount of cooking oil really saves calories and fat grams. *Every type of oil*—even the more healthful monosaturated varieties such as "light" olive oil and canola oil—*contains roughly 120 calories and 14 grams of fat per tablespoon!* Whenever possible, steam, roast, boil, or broil your meats and vegetables instead of frying.

— When cooking seafood, choose lower-fat varieties. In general, white fish contains fewer fat grams and calories than red fish. For example, a pound of rainbow trout contains almost 900 calories and over 50 grams of fat, while a pound of sole contains 310 calories and under 4 grams of fat.

Sample One-Week Dinner Menu Plan

Here is a sample meal plan consisting of seven dinners for you and your family to enjoy. All of the dishes are low in fat and calories, while delivering lots of taste, interesting textures, and visual appeal. I'll discuss breakfast, lunch, and snacks later.

❧ CRAB-STUFFED SOLE WITH LEMON CAPER SAUCE ❧

(Serves four; 152 calories, 4.5 grams fat per serving, including the sauce)

This elegant dish has a light, delicate flavor that will please everyone—from discriminating connoisseurs of fine dining, to kids who normally hate fish. It is light in calories, yet quite satisfying. Suggestion: Serve with baked potatoes topped with light butter, and steamed broccoli florets covered with the extra Lemon Caper Sauce.

Chicken broth, one 14.5-oz. can, clear and low-sodium
Garlic, 1 clove or ½ teaspoon, crushed
Onion, 1 medium brown, peeled and minced
Mushrooms, 2 cups sliced
Ground pepper, ⅛ teaspoon
Crabmeat, 6 oz. (¾ cup) fresh or canned (drained)
Filets of sole (4)

First, preheat oven to 325 degrees. Put ⅓ cup chicken broth in a large skillet, and put the remaining chicken broth in a medium sauce pan to make Lemon Caper Sauce (ingredients and directions follow). Heat the broth in the skillet over medium/high heat until it is simmering, and stir in the garlic. Stir for 2 minutes, then add onions, mushrooms, and the ground pepper. Allow mixture to cook for 5 minutes, stirring frequently.

In the meantime, slice each fish filet in half lengthwise, to form a top and bottom (as if making a sandwich). Place filet bottoms across the bottom of a nonstick or glass baking pan.

Returning to the skillet, add the crabmeat, and heat an additional 2 to 3 minutes, stirring gently to avoid shredding it. Spoon the mixture evenly over each filet slice, and cover with the top half of each filet. Cover the baking pan with aluminum foil and cook in preheated oven for 15 minutes, while preparing the Lemon Caper Sauce

Lemon Caper Sauce

Chicken stock, remaining
Butter or margarine, 2 tablespoons, low-fat
Lemon juice, ⅓ cup (fresh-squeezed tastes better, but bottled will do)
Dill, ¼ teaspoon
Flour, ⅓ cup
Capers, 3 tablespoons

Heat chicken stock in medium sauce pan over medium-high heat until it reaches a rolling boil. Using a wire whisk, stir in butter or margarine until it melts and mixture returns to a rolling boil. Add the lemon juice and dill, and stir for one minute. Slowly add the flour, one-third at a time, using the whisk continuously to give the mixture a smooth, uniform texture. Reduce heat to low, and stir the mixture frequently.

Remove the fish filets from the oven. Carefully add capers to sauce pan, and gently stir in. Place filets on serving plates, and pour the Lemon Caper Sauce over each serving.

❧ CHICKEN YAKI-SOBI ❧

(Serves four; 525 calories and 8 grams of fat per serving)

This take-off on a traditional Japanese dish may become one of your family's favorite meals. Not only is it quick, easy, and inexpensive to prepare, but it's packed with flavor and healthful, fill-you-up ingredients. Yaki-Sobi is a balanced meal all by itself.

Chinese or yaki-sobi noodles, 12 oz.
Chicken broth, low-sodium and clear, one 14.5-oz. can
Chicken breasts (4), skinless and de-boned, one lb. total
Soy sauce, low-sodium, 1 tablespoon
Ground ginger, ½ teaspoon
Garlic, ½ clove or ¼ teaspoon crushed
Ground pepper, ⅛ teaspoon
Red bell pepper, 1 cup minced
Mushrooms, 2 cups sliced
Scallions (green onions), ½ cup diced (including greens)
Chinese peas, ends removed, 1 ½ cups

Fill a very large pot with hot water and bring to a rolling boil. Add noodles and stir. After the water returns to a rolling boil, add ½ cup cold water and stir. Repeat this process—allowing water to reach a rolling boil, then adding ½ cup cold water and stirring for approximatel ⋅ 15 minutes—while you are preparing the yaki-soba sauce:

Pour chicken broth into a medium or large saucepan, and heat over medium/high heat for 2 minutes. Stir in soy sauce, ginger, garlic, and ground pepper. Add bell pepper and cover. (Remember to keep adding cold water to the boiling noodles).

Then chop chicken breasts into approximately 1″ x 1″ (bite-sized) pieces. Stir chicken into the chicken broth and bell pepper mixture. Cover and cook for 2 minutes. Add mushrooms, scallions, and Chinese peas, making sure all the vegetables are coated with chicken broth. Reduce heat to low/medium. After stirring mixture gently, cover and cook for 3 additional minutes. Mixture is ready when chicken is white throughout and the Chinese peas are slightly softened.

Drain noodles and place one-fourth of the noodles on individual deep-sided plates or large bowls. Pour one-fourth of the Yaki-Sobi mixture, including broth, over each serving of noodles.

❧ TURKEY CACCIATORE ❧

(Serves four; 304 calories and 6 grams of fat per serving)

This filling meal is so loaded with spicy flavor that your family may not believe it's low in calories and fat—and neither will you! Suggestion: Serve with a tossed garden salad with low-fat or fat-free dressing. This dish may also be served over noodles—the number of calories will increase by about 150 or 200 calories per portion, but the fat gram count will still be low. If you don't want noodles with the dish, you can serve it with fat-free muffins or sourdough bread as a complementary starch.

Turkey Breast, skinless and de-boned, approximately ¾ lb.
Carrots, 2 medium, sliced
Mushrooms, 2 cups, sliced
Brown onion, 1 medium, diced
Scallions, 1 cup, diced (white section only)
Red bell pepper, 1 cup, diced
Stewed tomatoes, two 14.5-oz. cans
Garlic, 2 cloves or 1 teaspoon, crushed
Oregano, 1 teaspoon
Basil, ½ teaspoon
Ground pepper, ¼ teaspoon
Thyme, ⅛ teaspoon
Marjoram, ⅛ teaspoon
Parmesan cheese, fat-free or low-fat, ⅓ cup
Mozzarella, skim or part-skim, 1 cup shredded

Preheat oven to 350 degrees. Place turkey and vegetables in a 9″ x 13″ baking pan. Cover with aluminum foil and place in refrigerator while you prepare the cacciatore sauce:

Pour the stewed tomatoes into a medium or large saucepan over medium heat. Stir in spices and garlic and keep stirring until mixture just begins to bubble. Reduce heat to low, cover, and allow to simmer for five minutes.

Next, pour cacciatore sauce over turkey and vegetables. Sprinkle Parmesan and mozzarella cheeses over entire mixture. Recover with aluminum foil and bake in 350-degree (preheated) oven for 45 minutes.

?◆ SALMON FETTUCCINE ?◆

(Serves four; 579 calories and 12 grams of fat per serving)

Who doesn't love fettuccine, with its rich creamy sauce? And when you add the delicate and distinctive flavor of salmon, you have a real dinnertime favorite. Traditional fettuccine, prepared with heavy whipping cream (50% fat!), real butter, and whole milk Parmesan, is, of course, incredibly delicious. But who can afford the fat, cholesterol, calories, and that heavy feeling of overeating? This low-fat version isn't as rich as the real cream variety, but it will satisfy your appetite for a smooth, creamy sauce! The meal is very filling and satisfying, yet light enough to fit into your weight-watching menu.

Cooking Utensils Needed:
Small (9" x 9") nonstick or glass baking pan
Large pot for boiling noodles
Medium-size pot
Vegetable steamer
Medium saucepan
Colander
Wire whisk

Ingredients
Salmon fillet, ¾ lb., de-boned
Garlic, 3 cloves or 3 teaspoons, crushed
Fettuccine noodles, 10 oz.
Mushrooms, 2 cups, sliced
Broccoli florets, 2 cups
Butter or margarine, 2 tablespoons, low-fat
Cream cheese, 3 tablespoons, fat-free
Milk, 1½ cups, nonfat
Parmesan cheese, ¾ cup, fat-free or low-fat
Flour, 1 tablespoon

Preheat oven to 425 degrees. Fill a large pot with hot water, and over high heat, bring water to a rolling boil. Add fettuccine noodles and reduce heat to medium, stirring frequently to keep noodles from sticking.

Spread one teaspoon of crushed garlic over entire filet of salmon (except the side with the skin on it). Place salmon, skin side down, in small nonstick or glass baking pan and cover with aluminum foil. Put in preheated oven (425 degrees) while preparing the vegetables and Alfredo sauce.

Put small amount of hot water in the bottom of a medium pot. Place vegetable steamer over water, and place mushrooms and broccoli in pot. Heat over high heat, with pot covered.

While the noodles, salmon, and vegetables are cooking, begin the Alfredo sauce: In a medium saucepan over low/medium heat, slowly melt the butter, stirring constantly. When the butter is melted, add the garlic, and stir until butter begins to simmer. Don't let the butter turn brown. Stir in cream cheese with a wire whisk, pushing the cream cheese around until it melts. Add nonfat milk and blend with wire whisk. Slowly whisk in ½ cup Parmesan cheese (reserving ¼ cup Parmesan for later use). When cheese is completely blended, slowly stir in the flour. Continue to heat, stirring frequently. Remember to stir the noodles, as well.

When the salmon has cooked for 12 minutes and the noodles are soft and no longer "gummy" (test by tasting one noodle), drain the noodles and put one-fourth on each plate. Spoon the vegetables over the noodles. Remove the salmon from the oven and slice the filet (without the skin) into several ½-inch-wide strips. Pour the Alfredo sauce over the noodles and vegetables. Place one-fourth of the salmon strips on each plate, over the sauce, noodles, and vegetables. Sprinkle one tablespoon Parmesan cheese on each serving.

❧ SMOTHERED HONEY-MUSTARD CHICKEN ❧

(Serves four; 299 calories and 6.75 grams of fat per serving)

This low-fat, low-calorie version of a favorite Southern dish will satisfy even the pickiest eater in your household. You'll enjoy the zesty combination of flavors, plus the ease of preparation. This is a meal you can make in a hurry and serve to your family often. Suggestion: This meal goes well with rice (one-cup servings of rice prepared without fat) or steamed new potatoes.

Chicken breasts, 4 skinned, boneless, approximately 1 lb. total
Scallions (green onions), diced, white section only
Mushrooms, 1½ cups sliced
Apple, 1 large or 2 small, peeled and diced
Butter or margarine, 2 tablespoons, low-fat
Honey, 4 tablespoons
Dijon mustard, 3 teaspoons
Flour, 4 tablespoons

Preheat the oven to 425 degrees. Place chicken breasts, scallions, mushrooms, and diced apples in large nonstick or glass baking pan, and cover with aluminum foil. Place in refrigerator while you prepare the honey mustard sauce:

In a medium saucepan, melt the butter slowly over medium heat, stirring constantly to prevent the butter from burning. Stir in the honey, one tablespoon at a time. Use a wire whisk to blend the sauce to a smooth consistency. Add the Dijon mustard, one teaspoon at a time, blending well with the wire whisk. Cook the mixture for two minutes, stirring constantly.

Immediately remove the baking pan with the chicken from the refrigerator. Pour the well-mixed honey mustard sauce over the chicken, scallions, mushrooms, and apples. Using a large spoon, gently mix the ingredients so everything is lightly coated with the honey mustard sauce. Cover with aluminum foil and cook in preheated 425-degree oven for 10 minutes.

Then remove the baking dish from the oven. Stir all the ingredients gently and remove the aluminum foil. Cook an additional 10 minutes.

Remove the baking pan from the oven. Using a slotted spoon, serve the chicken, topped with the vegetables and apples, onto each serving plate. With a wire whisk, add the four tablespoons of flour, one tablespoon at a time, to the honey mustard sauce left in the baking pan. When the sauce resembles a thin gravy without lumps, pour it over the chicken and vegetables, and serve.

❧ ANGEL HAIR PASTA WITH SHRIMP MARINARA ❧

(Serves four; 642 calories and 4.3 grams of fat per serving)

This is another low-fat version of a modern Italian dish. This is a favorite with my calorie-conscious dinner guests, who love flavorful, spicy food without the accompanying fat and calories. Suggestion: A Caesar-style salad is the perfect appetizer. Use shredded romaine lettuce and nonfat Italian dressing. Sprinkle with fat-free Parmesan, and you'll feel like you're eating a high-calorie feast!

Angel hair or vermicelli pasta, 16 oz.
Butter or margarine, low-fat, 1 tablespoon
Garlic, 3 cloves or 3 teaspoons, crushed
Brown onion, 1 medium, peeled and diced
Stewed tomatoes, two 14.5-oz. cans
Oregano, ½ teaspoon
Basil, ¼ teaspoon
Ground pepper, ¼ teaspoon
Thyme, ⅛ teaspoon
Marjoram, ⅛ teaspoon
Mushrooms, 2 cups, sliced
Red bell pepper, 1 cup, diced
Shrimp, one lb., peeled and deveined
Parmesan cheese, fat-free or low-fat, ½ cup

Fill a large pot with hot water and bring to boil to cook noodles.

In a deep-sided skillet or large saucepan, melt butter over medium heat. Add garlic and cook for one to two minutes, being careful not to burn the butter or the garlic. Add the onions, and stir until onion pieces are soft and transparent.

Stir in stewed tomatoes. Add spices and blend thoroughly. Bring mixture to a simmer, and add mushrooms and bell pepper. Reduce heat to low and cover, stirring frequently.

As soon as the large pot of water comes to a rolling boil, add the pasta and stir. Allow the pasta to cook, uncovered, at a low boil. Stir frequently to keep the pasta from sticking to the heat at the bottom of the pot.

Meanwhile, check to see if the mushrooms and bell pepper have softened. As soon as they appear soft, and the noodles also seem soft (but not gummy or mushy), it is time to add the shrimp. The secret of great-tasting shrimp is to cook them fast and briefly.

When you are ready to cook the shrimp, turn the heat on the saucepan to medium/high. Stirring continuously, add the shrimp. As soon as all the shrimp are pink on both sides, remove the sauce from the heat source.

Drain the noodles and divide into four servings. Pour the sauce, including shrimp, over each noodle serving, and top with Parmesan cheese.

❧ TURKEY VEGETABLE STROGANOFF ❧

(Serves four; 465 calories and 12 grams of fat per serving)

Here's a healthful way to enjoy stroganoff! The sauce is deliciously rich and flavorful, yet much lower in fat and calories than that of traditional stroganoff. Since you're serving it over vitamin-packed vegetables and low-fat turkey, you needn't feel guilty about enjoying it. As an added benefit, this meal is easy to prepare! Cook's note: This meal is made with low-fat sour cream, and I do not recommend substituting nonfat sour cream. I've tried three of the major brands of nonfat sour cream, and they all have a distinctive sour-lemony taste that doesn't do well in this dish.

1 lb. new potatoes (small red), skin on, cut in halves
2 cups broccoli crowns
2 cups mushrooms, sliced
1 lb. turkey breast meat, cut in approximately 2" x 1" strips
16 oz. low-fat (not nonfat) sour cream
1 teaspoon seasoned salt (without MSG), such as Lawry's
2 oz. feta cheese

Put a steamer basket in a large pot, and fill the pot with enough hot water to touch the bottom of the basket. Bring the water to a rolling boil, and put potatoes in the pot. Cover and let boil for 10 minutes. Add broccoli crowns, mushrooms, and turkey slices and cover to cook while you prepare the stroganoff sauce. Occasionally stir the turkey to ensure even cooking.

Put the sour cream into a medium-sized pot. Heat over medium heat, and stir in seasoned salt and feta cheese. Stir until the feta melts completely.

The dish is ready when the turkey turns completely white and the feta cheese has melted. To serve, put the vegetables and turkey on plates, and pour stroganoff sauce on top.

BON APPETIT!

CHAPTER SEVENTEEN

BREAKFAST, LUNCH, AND DESSERTS (ESPECIALLY CHOCOLATE!)

"Our minds create our future. When we have something in our present that is undesirable, then we must change our minds to change the situation. And we can begin to change it this very second."

—Louise Hay, author of
You Can Heal Your Life

ONE OF THE major goals of this book is to reduce your obsession with weight, eating, and food. I've outlined a sample dinner menu simply as a guideline for blending normal eating with light cooking. The meals I've suggested are carbohydrate-based, with an emphasis on pasta.

The other meals that you enjoy during the day can follow this same pattern. For example, in the morning, try to choose light but tasty variations on traditional breakfast meals:

- Nonfat yogurt with fresh fruit
- Fat-free granola with fruit and skim or 1% milk
- Fat-free muffins with all-fruit, sugarless jam
- Omelettes with scallions and mushrooms (skip the cheese)
  Note: This is a good choice when eating breakfast at a restaurant, where fat-free foods tend to be rare

- Fat-free caramel-flavored rice cakes or popcorn cakes, covered with mashed bananas or fat-free cream cheese
- Low-fat turkey instead of pork
- Fat-free cream cheese on fat-free bagels

Your lunch dishes can also be lighter versions of traditional meals:

- Sandwiches made with fat-free mayonnaise and low-fat meat and plenty of lettuce and tomatoes
- Vegetable or bean soups with a clear broth base, not cream-based soups (such as cream of mushroom or broccoli-cheese)
- Salads with low-sodium, low-fat dressings (avoid cheeses, nuts, avocados, and bacon)
- Steamed vegetables with fat-free salsa or salad dressing.

Snacks also follow suit. Get creative with healthy basics, and you won't feel deprived. Here is one of my favorite snacks:

❧ MOCK APPLE PIE ❧

First, dice one golden delicious apple in a small bowl. Then sprinkle it with ½ teaspoon each of cinnamon and nutmeg, and ⅛ teaspoon each of ground ginger and cloves. Cook it in the microwave on "high" for 3 minutes. Yum! It smells and tastes like apple pie and only has 85 calories and no fat. For "apple pie a la mode," top it with a scoop of fat-free vanilla yogurt (regular or frozen). To give it a "pie crust" and some crunch, sprinkle some fat-free granola over it.

How to Handle a Chocolate Attack

Chocolate cravings can send the most dedicated dieters into an eating binge! These maddening, seemingly out-of-control urges to eat chocolate occur at predictable times: during the menstrual cycle, winter months, holidays, and when we're craving love or reassurance.

I recommend counterattacking chocolate urges with two powerful weapons:

1. Keep your love quotient high. When we crave love, we're most apt to desire chocolate. The chemicals and feel-good taste of chocolate compensate for a lack of love in our lives. As I toured the country giving workshops and television appearances for my third book, *The Chocoholic's Dream Diet,* and I conducted psychotherapy sessions, I invariably found that chocolate cravings were connected to relationship issues. Self-love tools such as affirmations are extremely beneficial in combatting chocolate cravings. They fill you up with love feelings. Self-love means increased serenity, and this benefits your relationships, which will be more harmonious when you have harmony within.

2. Take the physical steps necessary to quiet your chocolate cravings. Here are some measures that help reduce chocolate attacks:

• Drink ginger ale or coffee. Both liquids contain chemicals similar to chocolate, and many people find that their chocolate cravings are diminished by the consumption of these beverages.
• If you consistently crave chocolate around the time of your menstrual period, keep high-fat chocolate out of your house during that time.
• Some chocolate cravings occur because the body craves adequate nutrition. If your diet is unbalanced or doesn't provide enough magnesium, calcium, or chromium, chocolate cravings can result. Magnesium deficiencies can also be triggered by drinking too much cola, since the cola leaches out magnesium from the body. A diet rich in these minerals comes from foods such as chicken, corn, and seafood.
• Chocolate isn't a "bad" food; it just contains a lot of fat and calories in the traditional forms of candy, cookies, and cake. However, I believe that a little chocolate in moderation is a good idea. If you completely deprive yourself of chocolate's wonderful taste and texture, you increase the likelihood of going on an all-out chocolate-eating binge. Instead of all-or-nothing, indulge in some moderate chocolate eating now and then.

• Instead of high-fat candy, cookies, pies, or cakes, try a nonfat chocolate treat! These recipes, from my *Chocoholic's Dream Diet* book, are desserts your whole family will enjoy. I think these snacks taste fattening, even though they're not.

❧ FAT-FREE DOUBLE-FUDGE COOKIES ❧

(Makes 3 dozen cookies; 50 calories and 0 grams of fat per cookie)

These delicious cookies taste as good as the fattening variety! They're gooey and very chocolatey, and will definitely curtail the cravings of even hardcore chocoholics.

1 cup all-purpose flour
½ teaspoon baking soda
½ teaspoon salt
3 tablespoons cocoa powder
¼ cup marshmallow cream
¼ cup dark corn syrup
½ cup granulated sugar
½ cup dark brown sugar
1 teaspoon vanilla extract
1 medium or large egg

Preheat oven to 375 degrees. Cook's note: I prefer to put aluminum foil on top of my cookie sheets and lightly spray them with nonstick cooking spray. By doing so, you avoid a lot of clean-up after baking; all you have to do is toss the aluminum foil in the trash!

In a medium bowl, stir the flour, baking soda, salt, and cocoa together. In a separate, larger bowl, mix the remaining ingredients. Slowly stir the dry ingredients into the second bowl.

Drop the batter into nickel-sized balls on the cookie sheet, leaving at least 3 inches between cookies. Bake for 10 minutes.

ೊ FAT-FREE CHOCOLATE CAKE COOKIES ೊ

(Makes 5 dozen cookies; 40 calories and 0 grams of fat per cookie)

Here's another favorite fat-free cookie recipe for people who prefer a cake-like consistency for cookies (the previous recipe makes very soft, gooey cookies). For those family members who aren't calorie conscious, this recipe makes wonderful double chocolate-chip cookies. (You can put chocolate chips in the cookies designated for non-dieting family members.) They'll be eating a lot less fat than normal chocolate chip cookies, without sacrificing taste and satisfaction.

2 ¼ cups all-purpose flour
1 teaspoon baking soda
1 teaspoon salt
6 teaspoons cocoa powder
4 oz. (½ cup) nonfat cream cheese
1 cup apple sauce (sweetened or unsweetened)
1 cup brown sugar
1 ½ teaspoons vanilla extract
2 eggs

Preheat oven to 375 degrees. Lightly spray cookie sheets, or aluminum foil over cookie sheets, with nonstick spray.

In a medium-sized mixing bowl, stir the flour, baking soda, salt, and cocoa powder together. In a separate, larger bowl, mix the cream cheese, apple sauce, sugar, vanilla, and eggs. Pour the flour and other dry ingredients into the cream cheese bowl. If you wish, add chocolate chips at this point, and gently mix.

Drop the batter onto the cookie sheet by the teaspoon, leaving at least 3 inches between cookies. Bake for 12 minutes.

❧ DOUBLE CHOCOLATE CHIP MILKSHAKE ❧

When I'm craving chocolate, I take the blender out of the cupboard and make one of these in a hurry!

One cup nonfat milk
2 tablespoons of honey or fructose (powdered fruit sugar)
¼ teaspoon vanilla extract
1 tablespoon unsweetened cocoa powder
1 square unsweetened baking chocolate
5 ice cubes

Mix all the ingredients, and blend on high for 1 ½ minutes, or until all the ice has broken down to a milkshake consistency. For variety, you can add one drop of flavor extracts: either peppermint, almond, coconut, butterscotch, or banana.

I also make it a point to keep lots of bananas and apples around the house for snacks. Bananas are especially filling, and they are certainly easy to fix. In fact, when I'm out grocery shopping and have the "hungries" on the way home, I'll eat a banana. Not only is it healthful with all its potassium content, it is also very filling, tasty, low-calorie, and fat-free!

Hot herbal tea in the evening is one of the best ways to quell late-night snacking urges. The hot liquid has a calming effect, lessening the temptation to eat as a result of tension or anxiety. Hot camomile tea with a little honey and skim milk practically tastes like a dessert, and it fills up the stomach sufficiently to make you feel satisfied.

Calories and Fat Grams: To Count or Not to Count?

Counting calories is a trap that makes you focus on food to such an extent that this practice may eventually drive you on an eating binge! I think all that weighing and measuring of food makes you feel deprived and restricted—feelings that can trigger overeating.

Even counting fat grams gets rather monotonous. A more realistic approach, one which can be adopted for a lifetime, is to estimate in averages. Stay aware of everything you eat, and make mental notes of those foods that contain fat. If you stay within the range of 25 to 30 grams of fat per day, your total caloric intake will automatically stay in the 1,250 to 1,500 range. This is a realistic target for a normal, healthy woman who wants to shed excess pounds. If she's moderately active with a regular exercise program, eating 1,250 to 1,500 calories per day will result in steady weight loss.

If you divide the 1,250 to 1,500 calories and 25 to 30 grams of fat over three meals and two snacks, you'll be able to eat plenty of filling, low-fat foods. Again, the point is to develop a realistic attitude toward food and weight loss. Develop a balance between feeling overly concerned about calories, and being in complete denial about your weight.

If your mid-afternoon and after-dinner snacks are fat-free, low-calorie foods (such as a banana!), you can divide 30 grams of fat between three meals. That's probably more fat than you could consume if you're eating "light"! Once you get in the light habit, you'll probably consume no more than 20 to 25 grams of fat per day. And your body's fat will melt off as your body seeks its true and natural weight.

The beauty of eating light, too, is that it naturally inspires you to eat a balanced diet. You'll find that you will seek out foods such as whole grain cereals and pastas, vegetables, and fruits, since they are lowest in fat. These foods, of course, are also those that are the most healthful for us.

Of course, a positive attitude is probably your best defense against any disease. As far as I'm concerned, eating light leads to a "light attitude." I feel better about myself when I'm eating light and exercising regularly, and I tend to let things that might normally lead to feelings of tension roll off my back. I feel more powerful and secure at such times, and I also sleep a lot more soundly.

A healthy lifestyle really makes sense, doesn't it?

WEIGHING IN—ASKING
FOR TROUBLE OR
FACING THE TRUTH?

"The greater part of our happiness or misery depends on our dispositions, and not on our circumstances."

—Martha Washington

MY PEERS in the eating-disorder field have been known to criticize my position on the concept of weighing oneself. Nonetheless, I stand by my advice, because I so firmly believe in it.

I think it's best that you weigh yourself every morning, right after you awaken and urinate. By doing so, you receive immediate feedback about your weight and eating habits, which allows you to accurately gauge your weight-loss efforts.

After all, how can you achieve a goal unless you are able to evaluate your progress? How can you abide by the speed limit unless your car has a speedometer to tell you how fast you're going? How can you reach a strange destination without a map showing you how to get there?

My peers tend to advise their clients to throw away their scales because "getting on them every day just places the attention on weight, which will make you hungrier and more focused on food." But while I understand the logic behind this advice, I don't think it works.

Please let me explain. You see, I'm really not advocating extreme reliance on the scale. I don't advise weighing yourself more than once a day, and I don't want the *quality* of any particular day to be dependent on what the numbers on the scale read. If your weight has dropped, it doesn't mean that you are a "good" person any more than a weight gain means that you are "bad." Weight fluctuations, after all, are normal. Salty diets, late-night eating, menstrual cycles—all of these factors can contribute to a change in the reading on the scale, without the body actually gaining fat. And some exercise programs actually result in heavier body weights because the increased muscle mass weighs more than the body fat.

I'm only advocating the scale as one element in your weight-loss assessment. Use it in conjunction with your other evaluation tools, such as noticing how you feel emotionally (energetic or lethargic), how your muscles feel (taut or soft), and how comfortable your clothes are (tight or loose). The answers to these questions can be combined with the information supplied by the scale to give you an accurate determination of your progress.

Some have found that without the feedback that a scale provides, it's too easy to return to old unhealthful eating habits that result in that yo-yo syndrome of up-and-down weight loss/weight gain. Many of my clients report engaging in the same behavior that Bonnie did for years:

> — Bonnie had gained and lost 20, 30, or 40 pounds more times than she could remember. Each time she'd lose the weight, she'd feel invincible. "This time, I'll keep it off!" she'd swear.
>
> In time, however, Bonnie's strict diet regimen would lapse, and she would return to her old eating habits. For example, she'd start using high-fat dressings again, and would pile nuts, bacon bits, and cheese on her "diet" salads. She would also apply extra butter to her bread, and cook with a fair amount of oil.
>
> But even though it was clear that her body was regaining the weight, Bonnie would deny facing the truth. Her clothes would feel uncomfortably tight, but Bonnie would shrug it off, rationalizing, "My clothes must have shrunk

in the wash." Also, she would only look at her face in the mirror while getting dressed in the morning, and, of course, she'd avoid getting on the scale.

Only months later, when none of her clothes fit, would Bonnie finally weigh herself. By then, she would have put on 30 pounds that she had to lose all over again.

Bonnie's case explains why I advocate daily weighing. Not only does it provide valuable feedback, but it keeps us from deceiving ourselves (which we're so skilled at doing!) about our eating and weight.

So, let me summarize some important information to bear in mind when using the scale as an evaluation tool:

• Weight fluctuations are normal. Factors such as water retention stemming from high-salt diets and menstrual cycles can dramatically affect your weight. So, too, can the time of day you weigh yourself. Our body weight can fluctuate up to eight pounds during the day, which is why a first-thing-in-the-morning weigh-in will give you the most accurate picture of your weight.

• Keep the scale in the same location every day. Weight readings can change if you move the scale from room to room (or even to different areas within the same room).

• Try not to weigh yourself more than once a day.

• Please don't measure your self-worth or determine "what kind of day you're going to have" based on the reading on that scale. If you have gained weight, then just use that information as a basis for taking the appropriate weight-loss steps.

• Your weight doesn't reflect whether you're a "bad" or "good" person; it is merely an indicator of how you feel about yourself. As you release your pain and self-blame, the numbers on the scale will bear witness to your "lighter" attitude.

And, trust me, that will feel so good!

KEEPING THE BODY
AND SPIRIT LIGHT

*"Your limits are defined by the agreement you
have made about what is possible. Change that
agreement and you can dissolve all limits."*
> —Dr. Wayne Dyer, author of
> *Your Erroneous Zones* and
> *Everyday Wisdom*

I'VE PROVIDED YOU with quite a bit of information in this book, all vital to the long-term success of your weight-loss efforts. Here is a summary of the most salient points:

1. Symptoms of unresolved pain include a seemingly out-of-control appetite for food, and body weight that refuses to stay off, in addition to other symptoms such as headaches, back or neck pain, insomnia, depression, cancer, heart problems, and gynecological problems.

2. To uncover the unresolved pain, you usually need to recall some painful experiences from childhood and/or adolescence and determine who the perpetrator was. If you blamed yourself for any abuse that you suffered, then you need to remind yourself that, as a young person, you weren't responsible for the abusive or neglectful actions of others—even if you somehow felt responsible at the time.

3. Your overactive appetite is actually triggered by one of these emotions: Fear, Anger, Tension, and Shame (FATS). When you feel hungry, you must avoid automatic eating and ask yourself if one of these four feelings is triggering the hunger.

4. You can use exercise, affirmations, and visualization techniques to transform the FATS feelings into Forgiving, Accepting, and Trusting your Self. An overactive appetite is a signal that you are not happy, probably because you're not fulfilling your divine mission or true purpose in life. You can effectively use your new tools to begin working toward your dream life.

5. As you feel more safe, secure, and confident, your appetite will naturally diminish. You will no longer need the shield that fat gave you, and you will no longer need to mask your pain with food. Your weight will naturally drop, since your body is meant to be normal in size.

6. You can release the pain, and you no longer have to hold on to self-loathing. You know that it's important to love yourself and the little girl inside you. You can turn your FATS feelings into a big "Forget All That Stuff" and leave the painful memories behind you. Memories serve a purpose—they help you realize why you were mad at yourself. But once you've done so, and have released your self-blame, you can forget about the past. You are not broken or damaged—you are whole and complete, because God made you in His image and likeness.

You Deserve a Light Life!

Right this minute, you're deciding on the size and health of your body. If you're reading this paragraph while exercising, drinking water, eating low-fat foods, or snacking on fruit, the sum total of your nutritional and exercise habits will show up on your scale every day. If you don't weigh yourself, the sum total is evident in other ways: your energy level, mood, and the way your clothes feel on your body.

Remember, I'm not asking you to deprive yourself in any way or to embark on a stringent diet. What I am suggesting is that you approach the issues connected to health and weight from a positive standpoint.

That is, discard the type of negative thinking that says: "I have to avoid bad foods," "I can't eat sweets or junk food," I have to lose weight; I'm so fat," and replace these thoughts with positive affirmations such as "It feels good to eat fresh, healthful foods," "I have so much energy when I eat fruit, vegetables, and whole grains," and "I'm choosing to live in a healthy, fit body."

And, please, let me leave you with one other important piece of information to "digest": No matter how good a piece of food tastes, the taste is fleeting and the fat is lasting. What certain dieting organizations profess in their meetings is absolutely true: "Nothing tastes as good as thin feels." Food is a quick-fix for troubling emotions and thoughts, but the results last about as long as a small bandage on a severed artery.

Listen to your food cravings—they are part of your inner voice and provide valuable information. Listen to your feelings—the more powerful and troubling they are, the more urgent their message is to you. Listen to your inner vision, where you will "see" the life of your dreams—this is the road map that will enable you to fulfill your life's mission. And when you fulfill your purpose, you also fill up any emptiness and insecurity. You'll no longer require excess food at that point.

My sincere wish is that you treat your body and soul with compassion and kindness. Love that little child inside of you, and be understanding when she occasionally falters. Give her lots of hugs and encouragement, and she'll reward you with lots and lots of smiles from deep inside of you—smiles that are more delicious than any food you could possibly eat.

I wish the very best for you! And please know that I will be with you in spirit every step of the way!

APPENDIX

CONFIDENTIAL READER SURVEY

I'm interested in learning more about the experiences that led to your "Pounds of Pain" so that I can better help my clients and readers escape the prison of overweight and emotional distress. Please take a few moments to answer the questions below on a separate piece(s) of paper, and then mail it to the address listed at the end of the survey. All of your responses will be confidential. Thank you!

1. Are you female or male?
2. What is your age?
3. About how old were you when you first felt overweight?
4. Explain the nature of your life at that time (who did you live with, what was your home life like, etc.?).
5. Were you abused or neglected as a child? If so, please explain.
6. Did this abuse or neglect affect your eating or weight? If yes, how so?
7. What is your life like today (relationships, health, weight, occupation, etc.)?
8. How does your present life compare with your dream life?
9. What steps are you presently taking to achieve your goals?
10. If all your wishes came true, what would your life look like in five years?
11. Have you achieved any of your goals through the use of visualization techniques or affirmations? If so, please tell me about your experiences.

Please mail your completed survey to:

Doreen Virtue, Ph.D., c/o The Editorial Director,
Hay House, Inc., P.O. Box 6204, Carson, CA 90749-6204

B I B L I O G R A P H Y

Abcarian, R., "Post-Quake Quirk Is Something to Chew On." *Los Angeles Times*, January 30, 1994, E-6–E-7.

Anderson, G. H. & Leiter, L. A. (1988), "Effects of Aspartame and Phenylalanine on Meal-Time Food Intake of Humans." *Appetite*, Vol. 11S, pp. 48–53.

Armsworth, M. W., (1990) "A Qualitative Analysis of Adult Incest Survivors' Responses to Sexual Involvement with Therapists." *Child Abuse & Neglect*, Vol. 14, pp. 541–554.

Beattie, H. J. (1988), "Eating Disorders and the Mother-Daughter Relationship." *International Journal of Eating Disorders*, Vol. 7, No. 4, pp. 453–460.

Behr, E. *The Complete Book of Les Miserables*. New York: Arcade Publishing, 1989.

Benward, J. & Densen-Gerber, J. (1975). "Incest As a Causative Factor in Antisocial Behavior: An Explanatory Study." *Contemporary Drug Problems*, Vol. 4, pp. 323–346.

Bowie, S. I., et al. (1990), "Blitz Rape and Confidence Rape: Implications for Clinical Intervention." *American Journal of Psychotherapy*, Vol. XLIV, No. 2., 180–188.

Bownes, I. T., et.al. (1990), "Assault Characteristics and Posttraumatic Stress Disorder in Rape Victims." *Acta Psychiatric Scandanavia*, Vol. 83, pp. 27–30.

Bricklin, M. (1993), "Destress Your Tummy Away." *Prevention*, Vol. 45, No. 11.

Burgess, A. (1985), "The Sexual Victimization of Adolescents." Washington, D.C.: National Center for the Prevention and Control of Rape.

Calam, R. M. & Slade, P. D. (1989), "Sexual Experience and Eating Problems in Female Undergraduates." *International Journal of Eating Disorders*, Vol. 8, No. 4, pp. 391–397.

Cattanach, M. & Rodin, J. (1988), "Psychosocial Components of the Stress Process in Bulimia." *International Journal of Eating Disorders*, Vol. 7, No. 1, pp. 75–88.

Cavaiola, A. A. & Schiff, M. (1989), "Self-Esteem in Abused Chemically Dependent Adolescents." *Child Abuse & Neglect*, Vol. 13, pp. 327–334.

Chaouloff, F., et al. (1989), "Physical Exercise: Evidence for Differential Consequences of Tryptophan on 5-HT Synthesis and Metabolism in Central Serotonergic Cell Bodies and Terminals." *Journal of Neural Transmission,* Vol. 78, pp. 121–130.

Chu, J. A. & Dill, D. L. (1990), "Dissociative Symptoms in Relation to Childhood Physical and Sexual Abuse." *American Journal of Psychiatry,* Vol. 147, No. 7, pp. 887–891.

Cohen, F. S. & Densen-Gerber, J. (1982). "A Study of the Relationship Between Child Abuse and Drug Addiction in 178 Patients: Preliminary Results." *Child Abuse & Neglect,* No. 6, pp. 383–387.

Cornell, W. & Olio, K. (1991), "Integrating Affect in Treatment with Adult Survivors of Physical and Sexual Abuse." *American Journal of Orthopsychiatry,* Vol. 61, No. 1, pp. 59–69.

Daie, N., et al. (1989), "Long-Term Effects of Sibling Incest." *Journal of Clinical Psychiatry,* Vol. 50, No. 11, pp. 428–431.

Devine, R. (1980). "Incest: A Review of the Literature." In *Sexual Abuse of Children: Selected Readings.* Washington, D.C.: U.S. Department of Health and Human Services, DHHS Publication No. (OHDS) 78-30161.

Dyer, J. B. & Crouch, J. G. (1988), "Effects of Running and Other Activities on Moods," *Perceptual and Motor Skills,* Vol. 67, No. 43–50.

Dyer, W. W., *Everyday Wisdom.* Carson, California: Hay House, 1993.

Felitti, V. J., "Long-Term Medical Consequences of Incest, Rape and Molestation." *Southern Medical Journal,* Vol. 84, No. 3, pp. 328–331.

Fernstrom, J. D. (1988), "Carbohydrate Ingestion and Brain Serotonin Synthesis: Relevance to a Putative Control Loop for Regulating Carbohydrate Ingestion, and Effects of Aspartame Consumption." *Appetite,* Vol. 11S, pp. 35–41.

Frankl, V. E., *Man's Search For Meaning.* Boston: Beacon Press, 1962.

Friedman, S. R. (1990), "What Is Child Sexual Abuse?" *Journal of Clinical Psychology,* Vol. 46, No. 3, pp. 372–397.

Friedrich, J. and Virtue, D., *Eat, Sleep and Be Sexy.* Envision Videos.

Gardner, R. M., et al. (1991), "Body Image of Sexually and Physically Abused Children." *Journal of Psychiatry,* Vol. 24, No. 4, pp. 313–321.

Goldfarb, L. A. (1987), "Sexual Abuse Antecedent to Anorexia Nervosa, Bulimia, and Compulsive Overeating: Three Case Reports." *International Journal of Eating Disorders,* vol. 6, No. 5, pp. 675–680.

Goldsmith, S. J., et al. (1992), "Psychiatric Illness in Patients Presenting for Obesity Treatment." *International Journal of Eating Disorders,* Vol. 12, No. 1, pp. 63–71.

Gordon, B. N., et al., (1990), "Children's Knowledge of Sexuality: A Comparison of Sexually Abused and Nonabused Children." *American Journal of Orthopsychiatry,* Vol. 60, No. 2, pp. 250–257.

Greenwald, E., et al. (1990), "Childhood Sexual Abuse: Long-Term Effects on Psychological and Sexual Functioning in a Non-Clinical and Non-Student Sample of Adult Women." *Child Abuse & Neglect,* Vol. 14, pp. 503–513.

Hay, L.L. *Heal Your Body: The Mental Causes for Physical Illness and the Metaphysical Way to Overcome Them (Revised Edition).* Carson, California: Hay House, 1988.

Hay, L.L. *You Can Heal Your Life.* Carson, California: Hay House, 1984.

Henriksen, S., et al. (1974), "The Role of Serotonin in the Regulation of a Phasic Event of Rapid Eye Movement Sleep: The Ponto-geniculo-occipital Wave." *Advances in Biochemical Psychopharmacology,* Vol. 11, pp. 169–179.

Kopp, S. *Raise Your Right Hand Against Fear!* Minneapolis: CompCare Publishers, 1989.

Ladwig, G. B. & Andersen, M. D. (1989), "Substance Abuse in Women: Relationship Between Chemical Dependency of Women and Past Reports of Physical and/or Sexual Abuse." *The International Journal of the Addictions,* Vol. 24, vol. 8, pp. 739–754.

Mackey, T. F., et. al. (1991), "Comparative Effects of Sexual Assault on Sexual Functioning of Child Sexual Abuse Survivors and Others." *Issues in Mental Health Nursing,* Vol. 12, pp. 89–112.

Marano, H. E. (1993), "Chemistry & Craving." *Psychology Today,* Vol. 26, No. 1.

Martin, S., et al. (1988), "Self-Esteem of Adolescent Girls as Related to Weight." *Perceptual and Motor Skills,* Vol. 67, pp. 879–884.

May, R., *The Meaning of Anxiety.* New York: W.W. Norton, 1977 (Revised Edition).

Morgan, E. & Froning, M. (1989), "Child Sexual Abuse Sequelae and Body-Image Surgery." *Plastic and Reconstructive Surgery,* Vol. 86, No. 3, pp. 475–478.

Mynors-Wallis, L. (1992), et al., "Life Events and Anorexia Nervosa: Differences Between Early and Late Onset Cases." *International Journal of Eating Disorders,* Vol. 11, No. 4, pp. 369–375.

Neergaard, L., "When It Comes To Fitness, Americans Prefer Lazy Way." *The Orange County Register,* November 7, 1993.

Ogata, S. N., et al. (1990), "Childhood Sexual and Physical Abuse in Adult Patients with Borderline Personality Disorder." *American Journal of Psychiatry,* Vol. 147, No. 8, pp. 1008–1012.

Oppenheimer, R., et al. (1985), "Adverse Sexual Experience in Childhood and Clinical Eating Disorders: A Preliminary Description.", *Journal of Psychiatry*, vol. 19, No. 2/3, pp. 357–361.

Paddison, P. L., et al. (1990), "Sexual Abuse and Premenstrual Syndrome: Comparison Between a Lower and Higher Socioeconomic Group." *Psychosomatics*, Vol. 31, No. 3, pp. 265–271.

Peale, N. V., *The Positive Principle Today*. New York: Prentice-Hall, 1976.

Pennington, J. & Church, H. N., *Food Values of Portions Commonly Used*, 14th Edition. New York: Harper & Row Publishers, 1985.

Peterson, S., "Weighed Down By Prejudice?" *Orange County Register*, September 30, 1993, 1–6.

Rand, C. & Kuldau, J. (1989), "The Epidemiology of Obesity and Self-Defined Weight Problem in the General Population: Gender, Age, and Social Class." *International Journal of Eating Disorders*, Vol. 9, No. 3, pp. 329–343.

Rohsenow, D. J., et al. (1988). " Molested As Children: A Hidden Contribution to Substance Abuse?" *Journal of Substance Abuse Treatment*, Vol. 5, pp. 18–18.

Root, M. P. (1989), " Treatment Failures: The Role of Sexual Victimization in Women's Addictive Behavior." *American Journal of Orthopsychiatry*, Vol. 59, No. 4, pp. 542–549.

Rosen, J. C., et al. (1990), "Life Stress, Psychological Symptoms and Weight Reducing Behavior in Adolescent Girls: A Prospective Analysis." *International Journal of Eating Disorders*, vol. 9, No. 1, pp. 17–26.

Schuman, M., et al. (1990), "Sweets, Chocolate and Atypical Depressive Traits." *The Journal of Nervous and Mental Disease*, Vol. 175, pp. 491–499.

Shapiro, S. & Dominiak, G. (1990), "Common Psychological Defenses Seen in the Treatment of Sexually Abused Adolescents." *American Journal of Psychotherapy*, Vol. XLIV, No. 1, pp. 68–74.

Singer, M. I., et al. (1989), " The Relationship Between Sexual Abuse and Substance Abuse Among Psychiatrically Hospitalized Adolescents." *Child Abuse & Neglect*, Vol. 13, pp. 319–325.

Smolak, L., et al. (1990), "Are Child Sexual Experiences Related to Eating-Disordered Attitudes and Behaviors in a College Sample?" *International Journal of Eating Disorders*, Vol. 9, No. 2, pp. 167–178.

Strober, M. (1984), "Stressful Life Events Associated with Bulimia in Anorexia Nervosa." *International Journal of Eating Disorders*, Vol. 3, No. 2, pp. 3–15.

Surrey, J., et al. (1990), "Reported History of Physical and Sexual Abuse

and Severity of Symptomatology in Women Psychiatric Outpatients."
American Journal of Orthopsychiatry, Vol. 60, No. 3, pp. 412–417.

Terr, L. C. (1991)," Childhood Traumas: An Outline and Overview." *American Journal of Psychiatry,* Vol. 148, No. 1, pp. 10–19.

Tice, L., et al. (1989), "Sexual Abuse in Patients with Eating Disorders."
Psychiatric Medicine, Vol. 7, No. 4, pp. 257–267.

Virtue, D. L., *The Chocoholic's Dream Diet.* First Edition: Bantam, 1990.
Second Edition: Century-Guild Press, 1994.

Virtue, D. L., *The Yo-Yo Syndrome Diet.* New York: Harper-Collins, 1990.

Virtue, D. L., *My Kids Don't Live With Me Anymore: Coping With The Custody Crisis.* Minneapolis, Minn.: CompCare, 1988.

Wallace, R., Survey: "Good Grades Don't Give Immunity From Sexual Assaults." *The Orange County Register,* December 1, 1993, 6(A).

Weingourt, R. (1990), "Wife Rape in a Sample of Psychiatric Patients." *Image: Journal of Nursing Scholarship,* Vol. 22, No. 3, pp. 144–147.

Wendel, G. & Lester, D. (1988), "Body-Cathesis and Self-Esteem." *Perceptual and Motor Skills,* Vol. 67, pp. 538–545.

Wurtman, J. (1982), "Studies on the Appetite for Carbohydrates in Rats and Humans." *Journal of Psychiatry,* Vol. 17, No. 2, pp. 213–221.

Wurtman, R. J. & Wurtman, J. (1988), "Do Carbohydrates Affect Food Intake Via Neurotransmitter Activity?" *Appetite,* Vol. 11S, pp. 42–47.

Young, E. B., "The Role of Incest Issues in Relapse." *Journal of Psychoactive Drugs,* Vol. 22, No. 2, pp. 249–257.

I N D E X

Subject Index

Abandonment 3, 21–24
  Fear of 93, 126
Abuse
  and depression 7–8, 13, 24
  Emotional and psychological
    abuse 13–25, 71–78
  Employer 47–50
  Neglect 14–18
  Psychological sexual abuse 70–78
  Ratio of men to women 7
  Self-abuse 55–58
  Sexual abuse 9, 83–94
  Statistics 7, 8
Acquaintance rape 107–110
Adult children of alcoholics 15,
    180–183
Adulthood weight gain 46
Affirmations
  How to make your own 35–36
  List of suggested af-
    firmations 140–142
Alcohol and Alcoholism 179–183
Anger 24, 31, 45, 93, 117–118,
    127–129
Anorexia nervosa 93
Approval, need for 16, 124, 173
Authority figures,
  fear of 16, 127
  sexual abuse by 100

Bariatric surgery 159–160
Body image 69–70, 79–82, 94, 136
Body memories of sexual
    abuse 88–90
Bulimia nervosa 71–72, 93

Calcium 169
Carbohydrates
  and cravings 130–131, 163–169,
    182
Chemical dependency
  in parents 15, 24, 180–183
  links to sexual abuse 93, 111,
    135–136, 181
  marijuana 104–105
  prescription drugs 15, 93
Child custody 26–28, 51
Chocolate
  cravings for 202–206
  mood-altering chemicals
    in 163–169
Chromium 169
Cola 177–178
Control issues 24, 39, 55–57, 67,
    78, 85, 94, 105, 111, 119,
    125–130, 151, 157, 160–161,
    173–174, 185–186
Cravings for food 163–169

Date rape 107–110
Depression 7–8, 13, 24, 50–53, 63,
    109–111, 135, 163, 213
Discrimination against overweight
    people 49–50
Dreams 41–42

Eating
  Disorders 3, 6, 8, 87, 93, 130–
    131, 180–181
  Emotional eating 63, 125–132,
    163–168

☙ 227

Author Index

Doreen Virtue, Ph.D., is a psychotherapist specializing in women's issues, especially those relating to weight and eating. The author of three self-help books, including the bestselling *Yo-Yo Syndrome Diet*, Dr. Virtue is a frequent guest on talk shows such as *Oprah, Donahue, Geraldo,* and *Sally Jessy Raphael.* Her articles have appeared in *TV Guide, Woman's Day, Complete Woman, Woman,* and *New Body* magazines.

Dr. Virtue's personal transformation from a "fat, unhappy, and uneducated housewife" into a bestselling psychotherapist with a fit, healthy body is testament to the information that she has presented in this book.

If you are interested in utilizing Doreen Virtue's services as a lecturer and therapist at workshops or other events, you may reach her by writing to her publisher: Hay House, Inc., P.O. Box 6204, Carson, CA 90749-6204; or by calling (310) 605-0601.

≈

We hope you enjoyed this Hay House book.
If you would like to receive a catalog featuring additional
Hay House books and products, or if you would like information
about the Hay Foundation,
please write to:

Hay House, Inc.
P.O. Box 6204
Carson, CA 90749-6204

or call:

1-800-654-5126

≈